WEALTH
IS A
CROWN

How to Experience Prosperity, Abundance, and Increase in Your Life

SHANE PHILPOTT

Unless otherwise indicated, scripture quotations are from the New American Standard Bible®, Copyright © 1960, 1962, 1963, 1968, 1971, 1972, 1973, 1975, 1977, 1995 by The Lockman Foundation Used by permission. www.Lockman.org.

All scriptures marked AMP are from the Amplified® Bible, Copyright © 2015 by The Lockman Foundation Used by permission. www.Lockman.org.

All scriptures marked AMPC are from the Amplified® Bible, Copyright © 1954, 1958, 1962, 1964, 1965, 1987 by The Lockman Foundation. Used by permission. www.Lockman.org.

All scripture marked BSB are from The Holy Bible, Berean Study Bible, Copyright © 2016, 2018 by Bible Hub. Used by permission. All rights reserved worldwide.

All scriptures marked CEV are from the Contemporary English Version® Copyright © 1995 American Bible Society. All rights reserved.

All scriptures marked ESV are from The Holy Bible, English Standard Version. ESV® Text Edition: 2016. Copyright © 2001 by Crossway Bibles, a publishing ministry of Good News Publishers.

All scriptures marked GNT are from the Good News Translation in Today's English Version-Second Edition, Copyright © 1992 by American Bible Society. Used by permission.

Scripture quotations marked KJV are from the King James Version of the Bible. Public domain.

All scriptures marked NKJV are from the New King James Version®. Copyright © 1982 by Thomas Nelson. Used by permission. All rights reserved. www.harpercollinschristian.com.

All scriptures marked NLT are from the Holy Bible, New Living Translation, copyright © 1996, 2004, 2015 by Tyndale House Foundation. Used by permission of Tyndale House Publishers, Inc., Carol Stream, Illinois 60188. All rights reserved. www.tyndale.com.

All scriptures marked WNT are from the New Testament in Modern Speech by Richard Francis Weymouth, published in 1903. Public domain.

Wealth Is a Crown: How to Experience Prosperity, Abundance, and Increase in Your Life
ISBN: 978-1-946180-24-7
Copyright © 2020 by Shane Philpott
Shane Philpott Ministries
1181 15th St. SW
Mason City, IA 50401
www.shanephilpott.org

All rights reserved. No part of this book can be reproduced, in part or in whole, without written consent from the author.

Cover and Text Design: Lisa Simpson
SimpsonProductions.net
Author Photo: Mikela Pischel

Contents

From the Author 7

Chapter 1: Hidden Wealth in Secret Places 9

Chapter 2: An Epiphany 19

Chapter 3: The Gold Is Good.. 33

Chapter 4: Wealth Creation 47

Chapter 5: Wealth Is a Crown 59

Chapter 6: The Strength of Wealth and the Sting of Debt 73

Chapter 7: The Master Key for Accessing Wealth 89

Chapter 8: The Seed and Stewardship..................................... 103

Chapter 9: Wealth Destruction and the Battle
    for Your Prosperity 115

Chapter 10: How God Defends Your Crown............................ 131

Chapter 11: The Power to Make Wealth 143

Conclusion... 157

Dedication

Wealth Is a Crown is dedicated to my children,

Josiah

Brianna

Keira

Liberty

Caroline

Johnny

Roman

Lily Anna

London

May you experience wealth, prosperity, abundance, and increase all the days of your lives.

From the Author

There are unchanging and eternal laws that govern biblical wealth, prosperity, abundance, and increase. These laws constitute a global system of wealth designed by God, from which He intended to radically and powerfully transform the lives of His people all over the earth throughout the ages. This wealth system, which has been operating successfully for thousands of years, is perpetual, predictable, powerful, and prosperous.

The journey toward understanding and mastering this system begins with revelation, which leads to inspiration, then to motivation, and eventually culminates in transformation. In short, it is a journey of extraordinary change! This change occurs as revelatory concepts, insights, and ideas regarding wealth come from God through the Holy Spirit to the church, unveiling divine strategies for transforming supernatural wealth into *super natural* wealth.

The Bible clearly demonstrates that all of God's children have been predestined and empowered to experience a life of abundance. Financial freedom, economic superiority, and victory over debt is not reserved for just a chosen few. According to Acts 10:34, God does not show favoritism or partiality, and He makes no distinction between one person and another. What the Lord did for Abraham, Isaac, and Jacob, He will do for you. What the Lord did for David, Solomon, and Paul, He will do for you.

Indescribable peace and joy accompany financial freedom, and achieving economic wealth and a life of prosperity should be more than just a dream; it should be a reality. If you have a desire to acquire a deeper understanding of the truths that encompass the powerful realities of biblical wealth, this book is for you.

I wrote *Wealth Is a Crown* so others might appreciate the true plan, purpose, and power of biblical wealth. My heartfelt desire is these insights might help equip Christians to both grasp and activate eternal economic laws that encompass heaven and earth, laws that have been engineered to simultaneously bless them while making them a blessing to others.

Ultimately, my desire is that God's sons and daughters would experience a vivid revelation of God's miraculous provisionary promises, a revelation that unshackles them from the chains of poverty and lack while strategically positioning them to be an economic powerhouse and force for good throughout the earth.

Shane Philpott

1

Hidden Wealth in Secret Places

I will give you the treasures of darkness
    And hidden wealth of secret places,
So that you may know that it is I,
    The LORD, the God of Israel, who calls you by
your name.

Isaiah 45:3

On January 26, 1905, the Cullinan Diamond was unearthed at the Premier Diamond Mining Company near Pretoria, South Africa. Since it was three times larger than any other diamond previously discovered, it was initially thought to be a worthless crystal. A massive 3,106 carats in its uncut state, the stone was just under 4 inches long, over 2 inches wide, and more than 2.5 inches high. It weighed over one pound and was as big as a person's fist. Thinking there was no way such an enormous stone could be a diamond, the mine superintendent assumed fellow miners had buried a large piece of glass as a joke. The management was so certain it could not be genuine that they directed the clerks to throw it out of the window.

But it was not a joke.

And it was not a fake.

The diamond was real.

After much persuasion, the gem was hastily recovered and authenticated. With its worth realized, the stone took its place as the biggest gem-quality, rough diamond ever discovered in the history of diamonds. The gemstone — considered a wonder of nature due to its exceptional size, blue-white color, and flawless clarity in its cut form — was named the Star of Africa. Shortly after its discovery, the Cullinan Diamond went on display in Johannesburg where it was viewed by thousands of visitors.

On October 17, 1907, Sir Thomas Cullinan, the owner of the mine, sold the stone to the Transvaal Provincial Government, which then presented the diamond to Britain's King Edward VII as a birthday gift. King Edward commissioned the cutting of the diamond to Joseph Asscher of the Asscher Diamond Company of Amsterdam. Asscher subsequently split the Cullinan Diamond into nine main pieces and ninety-six smaller stones of various cushions, pears, and marquises designs. The nine primary stones were labeled Cullinan I to Cullinan IX and went on to become the principal parts of the Crown Jewels of the United Kingdom.

The biggest stone, named the Great Star of Africa, is the largest cut, fine quality colorless diamond in the world. Its value alone is estimated at over two billion dollars. The pear-shaped diamond was subsequently mounted in the British Sovereign's Royal Scepter and Cross. The second largest stone was named the Second Star of Africa, and it sits in the Imperial State Crown, one of the monarchy's most valued treasures.

For decades these incomparable pieces have been displayed in the Jewel House in the Tower of London.

The seven remaining stones were set into numerous brooches, a necklace, and a platinum ring, respectively. These particular crown jewels of the Queen of England are held within the state rooms at Buckingham Palace. The Cullinan diamonds are believed to be the most visited objects in Britain, perhaps in the world.

In June 2012, as the complete Cullinan collection went on display at Buckingham Palace to celebrate Queen Elizabeth II's diamond jubilee, the exhibition curator stated: "Until January 26, 1905 no one had ever seen a diamond of this size. So incredible was its discovery that the moment it was found at the Premier Mine it was thrown out of the window of the mine manager's office because it was thought to be a worthless crystal."

The incredible story of the Cullinan Diamond seems almost too fantastic to be true. Even when the account is shared today, people raise an eyebrow and consider it with a mixture of skepticism and disbelief. Imagine the great waste it would have been had the diamond remained discarded. It would have been a tragic loss of beauty, magnificence, grandeur, and wealth. Forgotten and disposed of, it would have been crushed to dust along with the other rejected rubble, its true worth and value never recognized and celebrated.

The Pearl of Puerto

In August 2016, media outlets around the world began reporting the remarkable account of a poor Filipino fisherman who had kept a 75-pound pearl hidden beneath his bed. Making the story even more astonishing was the fact it had been stored there for over ten years. The priceless pearl, measuring one-foot wide and over two-feet long, easily dwarfed every other natural pearl that had been discovered. The details surrounding this amazing story subsequently captured the attention of journalists, gemologists, and oceanic researchers worldwide.

Approximately ten years earlier, the fisherman found himself stuck in the fishing waters off the Palawan Island coast in the Philippines. Having dropped his anchor during bad weather, he found himself unable to free it following the storm. Swimming down to dislodge the anchor from what was believed to be a rock, he discovered it was actually snagged on the shell of a giant clam. The fisherman hoisted the giant clam up from the ocean floor, extracted the gigantic pearl and returned with it to his thatch hut. Being a secretive man and having no idea of its value, he hid the enormous gemstone in a cardboard box beneath his bed in his home, keeping it as a simple good-luck charm.

A full decade later, the fisherman experienced a fire in his home. After moving out of the house, he gave the pearl to his aunt for safekeeping. Coincidentally, his aunt worked as a tourism officer for the local government in Puerto Princesa, on Palawan Island. "He'd almost forgotten everything about the pearl until he was moving out, and he remembered he had something under his bed," she said. She eventually convinced him to allow her to reach out to gemologists to certify the pearl's weight, value, and authenticity.

Following months of extensive research, a team of experts certified the pearl as one of the world's largest natural pearls from a giant clam. Christened the "Pearl of Puerto," gemologists estimated the rare pearl's worth at over $100 million. For over a decade, and unbeknownst to him, this poor fisherman was sleeping just inches from a great form of wealth which would ultimately transform his life. Vast and unimaginable wealth was hidden in a secret place in his home — within reach — for a good portion of his life. It took an unfortunate house fire to lead to the discovery of the vast wealth he had in his possession for so many years.

It's not difficult to envision the shock and disbelief experienced by that poor fisherman as he was instantaneously catapulted from poverty to wealth, all the result of a treasure that was kept in darkness. It was a life-changing moment for him as it would be a life-changing moment for anyone.

The Parable of the Lost Coin

Jesus told the people another story: What will a woman do if she has ten silver coins and loses one of them? Won't she light a lamp, sweep the floor, and look carefully until she finds it? Then she will call in her friends and neighbors and say, "Let's celebrate! I've found the coin I lost."

Luke 15:8–9 (CEV)

This parable, sandwiched between the Parable of the Lost Sheep and the Parable of the Prodigal Son, is one of three consecutive parables spoken by Jesus to those who had gathered to listen to Him. While the central thrust of these parables is the celebration that accompanies a repentant sinner, it is also important to note the illustration the Lord chose to use for His lesson was the search for lost wealth. The principles Jesus presented for reacquiring lost wealth in the Parable of the Lost Coin are illuminating, instructional, and insightful.

The parable begins with a substantial amount, ten percent, of a woman's wealth being lost, and describes her efforts to locate the missing coin. She immediately begins to search for the coin, taking all possible pains to locate it. Jesus describes her three-step process as:

1. Lighting a lamp.

2. Sweeping the floor.

3. Looking carefully.

The search for the lost coin is intentional, purposeful, and deliberate. There is no evidence of apathy or indifference. Nowhere in the parable is a lack of interest or absence of concern demonstrated. Rather, as the King James Version states, she begins to "seek diligently" until she finds the coin.

Diligence is an energetic and steadfast attempt to do something. It takes diligence to find that which is valuable yet lost.

Notice the thorough and deliberate method of the search. *Ellicott's Commentary for English Readers* says, "to 'sweep the house' can be nothing else than to use all available means for discovering the possible good that lies hidden or seemingly lost."

The lost coin, the Cullinan Diamond, and the Pearl of Puerto are all examples of good that lies hidden or seemingly lost. The Cullinan Diamond, while priceless by human estimation, pales in comparison when measured against the worth of God's promises. The Pearl of Puerto, so highly valued and celebrated by mankind, cannot hold a candle to the immeasurable value of the assurances of wealth and divine provision found in the Bible.

The Search Begins with You

These accounts bring into sharp focus that which has occurred with the wealth of many Christians, namely, how an object of such great value can be discarded or lost. Like those priceless gemstones, the realities of wealth have been thrown on the junk-pile, forgotten and lost in the darkness.

Discarded wealth is wasted wealth.

Neglected wealth is wasted wealth.

Forgotten wealth is wasted wealth.

Hidden Wealth in Secret Places

Hidden wealth is wasted wealth.

Wealth is of no use while it remains lost. For a moment in time, the Cullinan Diamond, a gemstone of rare and incredible value, lay on a pile of discarded rocks. Only after it was retrieved was its great value discovered.

The Filipino fisherman had in his possession a priceless natural pearl with no idea of its incredible value. It was discovered by him, just as it was lost by him. As a result, it became useless to him. Only after it was rediscovered did its great value become known.

Likewise, many Christians have in their possession priceless spiritual promises of incredible value that they have absolutely no appreciation of. One such possession is the revelation of wealth, which, if left undiscovered, will be equally as useless. And, like the fisherman, the years will pass with great wealth within reach, a promise waiting to be discovered, restored, and enjoyed.

Perhaps you identify with the mine superintendent who scoffed at the possibility of such a find while foolishly tossing the promises of wealth out the window. Maybe your spiritual experience has paralleled that of the natural fisherman. Either way, it's never too late to discover, or rediscover, your biblical rights to wealth.

It is easy to discard something so valuable when you do not know its worth. You may not realize it, but the Scriptures and promises of God regarding biblical wealth are the diamonds you have tossed or the pearls you have concealed. Be the one who begins the earnest search for the lost diamond. Be the one who begins the search for the lost pearl. Be the one who begins the search for the lost coin. That which is discarded or lost must be restored in order to be enjoyed!

You are on a journey to reclaim your discarded diamond.

You are on a journey to rediscover your lost pearl.

You are on a journey to find your lost coin.

You are on a journey to claim your wealth.

WEALTH RESTORATION

The concept of restoration is powerful. Restoration is the act or process of returning something to a former owner, place, or condition. However, the biblical meaning of restoration goes far beyond that. Biblical restoration means to receive back *more than* what was lost.

When God restores, whatever He restores is improved upon beyond measure, even to the point where the new state is greater than the original. He does it in such a way that it not only makes up for all of the losses, but He also gives His people more than they previously had. This is called a reward.

A large part of any victory you experience is the amazing realization of just how much God cares. This essence of God's ability to do abundantly beyond what we could even imagine is captured in the great Ephesians prayer:

> **Now to Him who is able to do far more abundantly beyond all that we ask or think, according to the power that works within us, to Him be the glory in the church and in Christ Jesus to all generations forever and ever. Amen.**
>
> **Ephesians 3:20–21**

The supervisor at the Cullinan mine and the Filipino fisherman both had something in common. They had no idea of the immense wealth that they held with their very hands. It wasn't until someone pulled back the curtain, unveiling the secret, and helped them to finally understand the value of their possessions. Only then, like the woman who searched for and found her lost coin, could they fully appreciate and utilize their previously unrealized wealth to the fullest.

Likewise, all of God's people are recipients of an incredible inheritance, a covenant bought and paid for by the blood of Jesus Christ. Discarding or ignoring this inheritance will only result in continued loss, lack, and poverty.

God told us in Isaiah 45:3 to expect to receive hidden wealth from secret places. He described this wealth as treasures, gifts that would serve as proof He had called us by name. It is impossible to exercise faith for that which we do not know is available to us. Consequently, we need to acquire knowledge regarding the origin, purpose, and power of the Lord's global wealth system so that we might not miss out on the enormity of His generous blessings.

> **By wisdom a house is built,**
> **And by understanding it is established;**
> **And by knowledge the rooms are filled**
> **With all precious and pleasant riches.**
>
> **Proverbs 24:3–4**

Taking Action

Application is the action of putting something into operation. In other words, this is where the rubber meets the road. It's time to take an inventory and usually the best place to start is by asking some questions.

A great question would be, "What are some valuable things I've thrown out the window?" While it may not be a huge, priceless diamond, it could be just as valuable. What about hard work, perseverance, and honesty? Have you considered the qualities of promptness, integrity, and diligence? These are all character traits that lead to wealth — traits that many people do not consider and simply pass by on their desperate search for a pile of cash somewhere.

Another good question is, "What could be in my life right now that I'm not taking advantage of?" The fisherman's priceless pearl was just underneath his bed! All those years he could have been making the most of its value, but he lived with great wealth within arms reach until a relative made the discovery for him.

What is in your house? Are there things that could be sold to launch a business? Is there a room that could be rented out, which might be the beginnings of your becoming a landlord? Are there collectibles you no longer want or need that could be liquidated in order to pay down some debt?

Then there is this question that God asked of Moses: "What is that in your hand?" While it was just a staff in the eyes of Moses, it was a tool for the miraculous in the eyes of God. What skills and abilities are you overlooking? Discovering and honing in on what you are good at will open multiple doors of opportunity. Is there a carpenter inside you, just waiting to get out? A programmer? An entrepreneur? A physician? It just might be the time to ask yourself: "What am I good at? Where do my skills lie? What comes second nature to me?"

It will take time, effort, and diligence, but no one else it going to do the search for you. God has promised to help you on your way to enjoying hidden wealth in secret places, but the journey must start with you!

2

An Epiphany

An epiphany is a moment of sudden insight or revelation. It is the unexpected perception of something's genuine nature. These revelations — or realizations — grant a person immediate awareness, comprehension, and knowledge on a particular topic. An epiphany is also described as the *aha moment*, the very instant when inspiration strikes.

I had such an experience while speaking at a church in New York City. This revelation was vivid, powerful, and remarkable. Later, upon reflection, it struck me as profoundly simple and clear. In what I can only describe as a flash of divine inspiration, this epiphany revealed to me a number of unseen and unknown dynamics related to the topics of biblical wealth, prosperity, abundance, and increase.

This was my *aha moment*.

This was my moment of clarity.

The topic for the service that morning was the glory of God's house. I was not speaking on the subjects of biblical wealth or economics, nor did I have any intention of doing so. The text for my message was taken from the Old Testament book of Haggai:

> **For thus says the LORD of hosts, 'Once more in a little while, I am going to shake the heavens and the earth, the sea also and the dry land. 'I will shake all the nations; and they will come with the wealth of all nations, and I will fill this house with glory,' says the LORD of hosts. 'The silver is Mine and the gold is Mine,' declares the LORD of hosts. 'The latter glory of this house will be greater than the former,' says the LORD of hosts, 'and in this place I will give peace,' declares the LORD of hosts.**
>
> **Haggai 2:6–9**

These Scriptures were very familiar to me. As a pastor, I had studied these verses many times throughout my years in the ministry. Yet while reading these verses aloud to the congregation that Sunday morning, the four words "the gold is Mine" struck me in an unforeseen and unexpected way.

A Divine Revelation

In describing the experience, I sensed I could suddenly see and understand the natural and supernatural connection between heaven, the church, and the wealth of the earth. It felt like an internal eruption of divine revelation. My heart and mind were instantly flooded with insight and comprehension. The entire incident affected me in a very unique and profound way and continued to do so for quite some time.

In the months that followed, I devoted much of my time toward sorting out what God had shown me. Each passing day brought with it more illumination and greater insight. Eventually, I began the process of organizing and arranging my thoughts. I wanted to be able to

An Epiphany

articulate what God had revealed to me, not just for my own benefit, but for the benefit of others as well.

Admittedly, I found myself reconsidering and readjusting my own attitude toward the concept of biblical wealth. I also found myself examining the motives and strategies needed for properly appropriating such wealth. I must confess I was somewhat shocked to discover I had been naively practicing much of what God revealed to me for years without fully realizing or understanding it at the time. I sensed that I had entered a season of enlightenment, and this epiphany was responsible for launching me on an extraordinary and rewarding journey of discovery!

It was a remarkable season. I invested considerable study, thought, and prayer into everything God was revealing to me. I was also reminded of Deuteronomy 29:29:

> **The secret things belong to the LORD our God, but the things revealed belong to us and to our sons forever, that we may observe all the words of this law.**
>
> **Deuteronomy 29:29**

Furthermore, Proverbs 25:2 states:

> **It is the glory of God to conceal a matter,**
> **But the glory of kings is to search out a matter.**
>
> **Proverbs 25:2**

I took both of these verses to heart as they promised wonderful blessings to any who would embrace God's revelations and to all who would take the time to search out the truths connected to them.

As the time passed, I continued to receive greater insight into the things God had shown me. The more I studied the subject of biblical wealth, the more understanding I received. Pressing in even deeper, I moved beyond simply examining my own personal core beliefs regarding wealth and began implementing real change in my thoughts and actions. I knew there were things I had not yet seen that God wanted to disclose to my heart.

It is a noble pursuit to seek the inner working of divine wealth. However, a serious study of wealth must first have certain ground rules established because of the obvious potential pitfalls connected to greed and wrong motives. It was clear to me that any revelation could actually be detrimental to a Christian who approached them without a firm foundation coupled with a balanced belief system.

Right Heart + Right Motives = A Firm Foundation

There are important truths that need to be agreed upon by those who aspire to understand and appropriate biblical wealth. In order for a person to be successful in their economic endeavors, these truths are paramount. The foundation for biblical wealth must be strong and secure.

First and foremost, it is crucial to note the topics of wealth, prosperity, abundance, and increase will never outweigh the preeminence of salvation and eternal life through Jesus Christ. We should always give our attention to what is most important in our lives and that, of course, is Jesus Christ. Nothing will ever compare to the priceless gift of salvation made available to mankind through the sacrifice and shed blood of God's Son. Everything else should be, and is, of much less importance. At no point should it ever be considered that wealth even remotely compares to the free gift of eternal life through Christ Jesus. The Apostle Paul said it best in 1 Corinthians 15:3–4:

> **For I delivered to you as of first importance what I also received, that Christ died for our sins according to the**

An Epiphany

Scriptures, and that He was buried, and that He was raised on the third day according to the Scriptures.

1 Corinthians 15:3–4

Additionally, while I personally believe the tithe — the tenth of our income that belongs to the Lord — remains a biblically-correct practice for today and have faithfully paid the tithe throughout my lifetime, my purpose is not to debate whether or not this commandment applies to present-day Christians. My personal opinion is the worst thing a Christian can do is to deny God access to any portion of the resources He has so abundantly blessed us with. This especially applies to the first and the best of our income, which is the tithe. When one reflects upon the gracious goodness of God and selfless sacrifice of Jesus, it seems such a monumental waste of time debating about whether a dime out of a dollar belongs to Him or not. Perhaps Jacob captured the heart of a thankful tither the best:

This stone, which I have set up as a pillar, will be God's house, and of all that You give me I will surely give a tenth to You.

Genesis 28:22

As Christians mature, they eventually realize they are the owners of nothing, yet stewards of everything. They come to understand the tithe is woefully insignificant when compared to the widow commended by Jesus in Mark 12:44 who, "put in all she owned, all she had to live on." They also know any monetary amount is inconsequential compared to the generosity of those in Acts 4:34 and 35 who willingly sold their homes and properties and brought all the proceeds from those sales to the apostles for distribution.

Furthermore in Acts 20:35, the Lord Jesus said, "It is more blessed to give than to receive." To a Christian, that verse is self-explanatory.

Giving is not tithing, as it is an entirely different financial transaction and method of worship. There are many today who, for whatever reason, have exempted themselves from giving, thereby disallowing the Bible from exerting any positive influence on their financial decisions and economic matters. Those who have conveniently excused themselves from the opportunities of presenting their finances to God have removed a key part of the prosperity equation. The truths and revelations pertaining to wealth, prosperity, abundance, and increase are specifically designed to assist only those who have a willingness to give, and this willingness is demonstrated through a heart and a history of giving.

A wise Christian understands that insights, strategies, and formulas regarding wealth acquisition will only be a mere supplement to the reader who has first put his or her complete trust and dependence in the Bible, God's Word to mankind. The Bible contains numerous scriptures that thoroughly address the issues of wealth, prosperity, abundance, increase, giving, receiving, sowing, reaping, sacrifice, partnering, investing, tithing, and offering.

Likewise, the Bible also includes scriptures that tackle the topics of robbery, thievery, poverty, destitution, insufficiency, hardship, financial ignorance, suffering and lack. And while many passages of Scripture connected to wealth may be couched in cultures and dispensations from long ago, they are far from obsolete. While we should be grateful for any revelation that addresses the biblical dynamics of wealth, prosperity, abundance, and increase, we should only receive those revelations to the extent they compliment and reinforce the Bible.

Finally, my purpose here is to deal strictly with material wealth. We understand there are many other definitions of "wealth" such as contentment, knowledge, health, happiness and so on and so forth. That being said, the subject of material wealth is what God specifically dealt with me about. The study of the acquisition of material wealth in no way diminishes other forms of wealth. Indeed, it will actually magnify our understanding of other forms of wealth when done properly and biblically.

Do You See Stars or Bars?

One of the world's most famous paintings, *The Starry Night*, is regarded as one of Vincent van Gogh's finest works and is instantly recognizable because of its unique and memorable style. Created in June 1889, the masterpiece is an abstract landscape painting of a swirling, star-filled night sky over a small hillside village. While millions of people have appreciated and adored Van Gogh's painting, few know the story behind how the historical piece of artwork came into existence.

Following a nervous breakdown in December 1888 that resulted in self-mutilation and loss of his left ear, Van Gogh voluntarily admitted himself into an asylum for the insane. Van Gogh stayed at the asylum, which was a former monastery, for approximately one year. It was during this season that he produced some of the best-known works of his career. Historians have identified the scene of *The Starry Night* as the view from Van Gogh's east bedroom window.

In May 1889, Van Gogh wrote a letter to his brother Theo and described the view: "This morning I saw the countryside from my window a long time before sunrise with nothing but the morning star, which looked very big through the iron-barred window." It was through this eastern window, he brilliantly captured the night scene that included a bright yellow crescent moon and eleven swirly stars spread out over rolling hills with a quaint, moonlit town set behind the dark green silhouette of a cypress tree. The painting, which is almost dreamlike in nature, has inspired and moved people for generations.

But there was one particular item Van Gogh chose to leave out of his unforgettable painting.

He left out the iron bars.

The ability to survey and appreciate the landscape beyond the bars necessitates a higher level of spiritual sight and thought. Society has projected their restrictive expectations and views regarding wealth onto Christians, and the majority of them have swallowed Satan's lies without question. What are these lies? Wealth is evil. Poverty is God's will. Prosperity is dangerous. Being poor blesses God. Wealthy Christians are thieves driven by greed. The list goes on and on.

What do you believe?

Do you see the stars or the bars?

The jealous and envious in this world have projected their expectations and limitations onto a church that deserves neither. The financial opinions and standards of the secular world serve as iron bars between Christians and their biblical promises. God's children must train themselves to see the stars beyond the bars in order to paint an unlimited financial future for their lives.

A Vanquished Vision

A perfect example of those who allowed themselves to be shut out by bars of their own making were the Israelites. Following their deliverance from Pharaoh's hand and the land of Egypt, God miraculously brought the people of Israel to the very cusp of the land He had promised them:

> **Then Caleb quieted the people before Moses and said, "We should by all means go up and take possession of it, for we will surely overcome it." But the men who had gone up**

An Epiphany

> **with him said, "We are not able to go up against the people, for they are too strong for us." So they gave out to the sons of Israel a bad report of the land which they had spied out, saying, "The land through which we have gone, in spying it out, is a land that devours its inhabitants; and all the people whom we saw in it are men of great size. "There also we saw the Nephilim (the sons of Anak are part of the Nephilim); and we became like grasshoppers in our own sight, and so we were in their sight."**
>
> Numbers 13:30–33

The Israelites allowed their sight to become fixed on the giants in the land. This failure contaminated their vision and corrupted their attitude. Ultimately, as a result of their negative attitude, the strategy God had given them for victory was negated. Their "bad report" not only cost them their possession of the Promise Land, but it also irreparably affected their own image of themselves. They believed they could not, therefore they did not, and an entire generation suffered as a result of their decision. The Israelites saw themselves through the eyes of their opposition rather than through the eyes of their God.

The picture they painted of the Promise Land included iron bars.

Likewise, Christians by the multitudes have fixed their eyes on the world's restrictions rather than God's promises, shutting themselves off from their biblical wealth. They have allowed the secular world to dictate their levels of wealth, prosperity, abundance, and increase. They see themselves through the eyes of worldly religions and dead denominations rather than through the eyes of "Him who is able to do far more abundantly beyond all that we ask or think, according to the power that works within us" (Ephesians 3:20).

The Israelites allowed their promise to be stolen from them, actually becoming complicit in the loss. Christians cannot afford to do the same with the Bible's promises of divine provision.

The Need for a New Mindset

A mindset is a mental attitude or disposition that determines how a person interprets and responds to situations. An individual's mindset will affect every area of their life.

After a serious study of Scripture, you may quickly discover the need to reconsider your attitude toward wealth. Obtaining a deeper understanding of the dynamics of biblical wealth will require a radical change in your viewpoint, possibly calling for a different mindset altogether. Changes in your attitude and thought life will culminate in changes to your strategies and results.

A person's manner of thinking will be reflected in their attitude, which will ultimately manifest in their actions. Attitude is a powerful thing because it affects a person's beliefs, stances, mood, and outlook on virtually everything. Attitudes are very hard to change because they become so deeply engrained in the person's thinking process that they become a part of that person's personality.

Cognitive dissonance is the state of having thoughts, beliefs, or attitudes that are inconsistent with our actions. Specifically, it is when our beliefs do not line up with our behaviors and decisions. This feeling of mental discomfort is common when an attitude or belief is challenged or altered. However, these attitudes toward wealth must be challenged and changed because the result will be the difference between abundance and lack.

An Epiphany

An attitude is a set way of looking at something, and the responses that accompany that view. Quite simply, an attitude is the way you feel about something.

Even though much of what you are reading right now might seem foreign or challenging to you, be patient. The process of changing your mindset will take faith, time, and effort. But it will all come together, and you will be rewarded in the end.

Your attitude toward wealth will change when your thoughts change, and your thoughts will change as a result of you thinking and meditating on the right things. The Apostle Paul addressed the importance of right thinking when he wrote to the churches at Philippi and Rome:

> **For the rest, brethren, whatever is true, whatever is worthy of reverence and is honorable and seemly, whatever is just, whatever is pure, whatever is lovely and lovable, whatever is kind and winsome and gracious, if there is any virtue and excellence, if there is anything worthy of praise, think on and weigh and take account of these things [fix your minds on them].**
>
> **Philippians 4:8 (AMPC)**

> **And do not be conformed to this world, but be transformed by the renewing of your mind, so that you may prove what the will of God is, that which is good and acceptable and perfect.**
>
> **Romans 12:2**

Approximately 1,500 years before Paul penned the words of Philippians 4:8 and Romans 12:2, God addressed the same principle with Joshua:

> **This book of the law shall not depart from your mouth, but you shall meditate on it day and night, so that you may be careful to do according to all that is written in it; for then you will make your way prosperous, and then you will have success.**
>
> **Joshua 1:8**

In order for Christians to experience success regarding biblical wealth, prosperity, abundance, and increase, their attitudes must change. They must change their attitudes toward biblical wealth before their strategies for acquiring wealth will ever change. As the popular saying goes, "Nothing changes if nothing changes."

A New Level

A bias is a preconceived and often unreasoned opinion about someone or something. Our biases will strongly affect our decision-making when it comes to our perception of wealth. Our biases will also affect our attitude toward wealth, or how we react to it. Our perception and attitude must change in order for our behavior to change, and when our behavior changes, new levels of blessing instantly begin to manifest!

God's Word is a hammer that chips away at our biases, removing error and shaping our motives, granting us the ability to open our hearts to the truths regarding wealth, prosperity, abundance, and increase. It is only when God's Word is allowed to correct our error and shape our motives that our mind will fully open to the power, provision and providence of wealth!

Taking Action

Ask yourself this important question: "Are my motives for wealth, prosperity, abundance, and increase right?" You must be brutally

An Epiphany

honest with yourself. God knows. There is nothing more frustrating and counterproductive than a Christian trying to get rich for all the wrong reasons.

Don't be afraid to get your heart right with God. Take time to examine your motives. An ulterior motive is an alternative reason for doing something, especially when concealed. You might be able to fool others, and you may even be able to fool yourself, but you will never fool God.

The next thing to deal with after getting your motives in line is getting your attitude in line. It will be next to impossible to change your attitude toward biblical wealth if you continue to feed yourself thoughts of poverty, lack, and insufficiency.

If you are truly serious about going to a new level, you will quickly discover the need for some changes in your life. There is a saying, "Garbage in, garbage out." This phrase is used to express the idea that the quality of output is determined by the quality of input. Let's be honest, if you're going to make the transition up to a new level of wealth in your life, it's going to have an effect on what books you are reading, who you are spending time with, and how much you are asleep on the couch.

You need your own epiphany. You need your own *aha moment*. You need your own moment of clarity. You need to paint your own picture without the iron bars. Go do it.

3

THE GOLD IS GOOD

While speaking in New York on that sunny April morning, I read aloud these words from Haggai 2:8: "… the gold is Mine …"

It was a singular moment for me.

I sensed I was on the threshold of understanding something very important. Yet, at the same time, I was somewhat confused. Personally, I had never been particularly interested in gold or desirous of owning it. Except for my watch and wedding ring, I certainly did not own any substantial amount of gold. I was not a collector of gold coins or gold bars. I did not follow the gold market or invest in any precious metals or commodities. Still, the scripture invaded my consciousness and dominated my thoughts.

I envisioned God physically standing in front of me and saying, "The gold is Mine." Sometimes I like to use this method of studying scripture because it makes the words personal and helps in my understanding. I do not believe this short statement recorded in Haggai 2:8 was simply to inform His people of something they did not know.

God's people already knew everything belonged to the Lord. Psalm 89:11 states:

> **The heavens are Yours, the earth also is Yours;**
> **The world and all it contains, You have founded them.**
>
> **Psalm 89:11**

This same thought is reiterated to the New Testament church in 1 Corinthians 10:26:

> **For the earth is the Lord's, and the fullness thereof.**
>
> **1 Corinthians 10:26 (KJV)**

In Haggai 2, God connected physical gold to the wealth of the nations, the glory of His house, and the peace that accompanies God's glory. Contextually, it is important to remember His words were a part of a prophecy given through Haggai the prophet to Zerubbabel, who was the governor of Judah at the time. The prophecy was likewise directed to Judah's high priest, Joshua, and also to the remnant of God's people. The central purpose of the prophecy was to encourage them in the rebuilding of the temple. So when God said, "The gold is Mine," He was reminding His people of a fact they had either forgotten or were in imminent danger of forgetting.

Pay close attention to the words in verse 5:

> **As for the promise which I made you when you came out of Egypt, My Spirit is abiding in your midst; do not fear!**
>
> **Haggai 2:5**

This verse hearkens back to the days of the Exodus when Moses led the children of Israel out from underneath the whips of their

Egyptian captors. When God commissioned Moses with his mission of deliverance, an essential part of that mission was the plundering of the Egyptians' gold.

> **I will grant this people favor in the sight of the Egyptians; and it shall be that when you go, you will not go empty-handed. But every woman shall ask of her neighbor and the woman who lives in her house, articles of silver and articles of gold, and clothing; and you will put them on your sons and daughters. Thus you will plunder the Egyptians.**
>
> **Exodus 3:21–22**

Scripture is carefully ordered by God, and it is not coincidence that the Lord referenced the account of the Exodus. Israel's deliverance and departure from Egypt involved the plundering of Egypt's gold. Later in the book of Haggai, the Lord connected that historical event to the wealth of the nations and the future glory of God's house. God also spoke of the peace that would come as a result of these events. It was not an accident that God spoke so highly of gold in relation to His temple. And it is in the midst of these passages that addressed hope, prosperity, and encouragement that God said, "The gold is Mine."

This heavy emphasis on gold is central to the revelation of biblical wealth and demands a deeper investigation.

THE ORIGINS OF GOLD

People are often surprised to hear that gold was not original to the earth. Scientists from the National Aeronautics and Space Administration, along with leading physicists at Stanford and Yale, discovered gold is actually a chemical element formed in outer space. Gold's formation is the result of supernova events or deep space stellar collisions of neutron stars. It is believed all the gold present throughout the universe today was created during these cataclysmic events.

One way gold is created is during an astronomical event known as a supernova. When certain stars die and the conditions are right, a small fraction of these stars will explode and produce a supernova, which is the catastrophic and dramatic destruction of a doomed star. A supernova event occurs about every fifty to one hundred years in a galaxy the size of the Milky Way. A supernova is the last stage of a star's life and is marked by one final and gigantic explosion. Such explosions are so massive and bright, they can be seen in other galaxies that are thousands of light years away.

Another way gold is created is during the collision of two neutron stars. Neutron stars, which are the collapsed cores of larger stars, are the smallest and densest of stars. A neutron star collision produces thousands of times more gold than a supernova, but occurs much less often. When two neutron stars collide, a massive amount of energy is released creating gold along with many other heavy elements found in the universe. So gold is a transition metal created in part by the explosive energy of gamma-ray bursts.

In a neutron star collision that just became visible to astronomers in August 2017, it is estimated the event produced 10 to 100 times the earth's mass in pure gold. Vast amounts of gold are created during these fascinating stellar events.

These violent supernovas and stellar collisions from the past jettisoned matter into deep space and, as a result, this ancient gold was present at earth's creation. In addition to the gold deposited in the planet's interior and core, the majority of the accessible gold located on the planet's outer mantle is the result of subsequent meteor bombardments. These meteors brought with them additional deposits of gold to the earth, likely arriving long after the planet was formed.

Through extensive measurements of the isotopic mixes of gold in rocks the scientific community was able to determine the origins of gold. The gold that is present upon the earth today, whether it be in nuggets and grains or rocks and veins, travelled here from the heavens long ago.

Whether present during the earth's creation or arriving later through meteor bombardments, gold is truly an out-of-this-world substance. Unlike diamonds, jewels, or other precious gemstones, gold is a heavenly material not produced on this planet. Whether forged in the nuclear fusion of supernova explosions or created in the atomic fire of neutron star collisions, this celestial metal is as amazing — and ancient — as the universe itself.

THE UNIQUENESS OF GOLD

Gold is an exceedingly rare substance. It is estimated that approximately 250,000 metric tons of gold have been discovered to date with about two-thirds of that having been mined since 1950. Most of that gold has come from just three countries: China, Australia, and South Africa. According to the United States Geological Survey, the entire global supply of gold — which some argue is the amount of gold mined since the Egyptians began mining it around 2000 BC — would easily fit into four Olympic-sized swimming pools.

The chemical symbol for gold is *Au*, which is derived from the Latin word *aurum*, which means *shining* or *glowing dawn*. It is called the king of metals and exists everywhere upon the earth in various concentrations. It can be found on every continent, in the oceans, and even in the atmosphere. According to the American Museum of Natural History, gold is even found within the human body, coursing through the bloodstream, with the highest concentrations located in and around the heart. Interestingly, gold plays an important role in the health and maintenance of the joints as well as being a key element of electrical signals throughout the body.

Gold is a remarkable, unique, and unusual substance. It is beautiful, durable, and extremely hard to find. The properties of gold will not permit it to rust or tarnish. It is the most noble of the noble metals, meaning it is resistant to both corrosion and oxidation, enabling it to shine forever. Gold is an eternal metal that does not react with oxygen at any temperature and is unaffected by most acids known to man.

This amazing metal cannot be destroyed by fire and only becomes purer when subjected to the intense heat of refining. It will not melt until it reaches approximately 2,000 degrees Fahrenheit, and it will not boil until it reaches approximately 5,000 degrees Fahrenheit. Gold is dense, but soft, incomparable in its luster and prized for its rarity.

Gold is also exceptionally malleable, meaning it is a pliable material capable of being hammered and shaped permanently without breaking or cracking. A single gram of gold can be beaten into a sheet measuring almost 11 square feet, and one ounce can be hammered into a sheet almost 100 square feet. It is ductile, meaning it can be drawn out into the thinnest wire. Just one ounce can be drawn into a fine wire 50 miles long. Gold can be pressed into a semi-transparent sheet so thin it will allow light to shine through. A gold leaf at only seven millionths of an inch thick would require a stack of over 7,000 sheets to achieve the thickness of a dime.

This amazing metal has been used as thread for embroidery, treatments for medical conditions, and thermal protection for the suits and helmets of astronauts. It is an excellent conductor of electricity and is used in the fabrication of corrosion-free electrical connectors in computers and many other electrical devices. Gold is also an essential industrial metal that enables critical functions to be performed in communications equipment, jet aircraft engines, and spacecraft as well as a host of other products.

As a result of its flexibility, purity, and inherent beauty, gold is highly sought after for its use in jewelry. People have adorned themselves with gold throughout the centuries, and every civilization since antiquity has mined gold and utilized it in statues, coinage, monuments, and sculptures. Gold is — and has always been — the eternal symbol of wealth and prosperity.

All civilizations of mankind, along with the earliest humans, have intuitively placed a high value on gold, equating it with power, beauty, and wealth. Gold is widely distributed throughout the earth, although in very rare amounts. This has resulted in a global attitude toward gold that been evident throughout the planet's civilizations both ancient and modern. The Book of Job refers to the refining of gold in Job 28:1: "Surely there is a mine for silver and a place where they refine gold." Gold was valuable to people on every continent, and even before it was used as the basis for money, it was considered a desirable commodity in and of itself. The value of gold is accepted globally and has been since it was first discovered.

These are just some of the amazing characteristics of the precious, heavenly-created substance called gold; the metal that God claimed as His own.

God's Chosen Metal

In the beginning God created the heavens and the earth.

Genesis 1:1

As the planet's Designer and Creator, the presence of gold upon the earth was planned by God. Though it sounds like science fiction, gold has been scientifically proven to be a heavenly material that was chemically forged in the cores of dying stars. It was during these celestial events that God infused gold with all of its amazing characteristics. He did this knowing humanity would recognize, appreciate, and value gold for its rarity and uniqueness.

Gold is a one-of-a-kind substance that God specifically chose to deposit into the earth. It was placed all over the planet in various concentrations and with varying difficulties of access. And like everything else in the world, it can either be used and enjoyed or abused and misused. Historically – and providentially – our planet was literally infused and sprinkled with deposits of gold. This is why astrophysicists say the planet was "seeded" with gold.

When God seeded the earth with gold, He introduced a form of wealth that had liquidity, mobility and security. It was the wellspring of wealth and subsequently became a store of wealth. Gold was the beginning of the earth's economies.

It cannot be emphasized enough that gold — the origin for the earth's global wealth reserves — was not native to this planet. This is why God could say, "The gold is Mine." Gold is God's metal, chemically forged in the heavens through exceedingly rare and ancient violent celestial events. Subsequently, God literally financed our planet's past, present, and future with gold. It is God's custom-designed, not-of-this-world wealth dynamo, the driving force that every economic and financial transaction springs from.

Earth's Global Wealth Engine

When God said, "The gold is Mine," He was saying, "The global wealth system is Mine." God has rightly claimed ownership of the earth's entire financial and economic wealth system. He could say this because He is the Architect and Designer of wealth. He is the Creator, Sower, and Distributor of wealth. Gold is God's universal form of wealth, created in the heavens, which brought with it the power to birth and perpetually sustain the entire planet's economic system.

Gold, which is divine in nature, became the cradle for the planet's global wealth engine, making God the Depositor, the Investor, the Banker and the Interest Payer. Gold was the genesis of every wealth system on the planet.

A Store of Wealth

According to Genesis 2, God told His people where He had created a store of wealth:

> **Now a river flowed out of Eden to water the garden; and from there it divided and became four rivers. The name of the first is Pishon; it flows around the whole land of Havilah, where there is gold. The gold of that land is good; the bdellium and the onyx stone are there.**
>
> **Genesis 2:10–12**

God placed gold upon the earth to be both discovered and mined. When God deposited gold, He installed the world's entire store of economic wealth. This store of wealth became the foundation for earth's perpetual wealth engine. This wealth engine birthed and sustains the entire planet's monetary and economic systems and has done so from the earliest of times. Literally, all of the planet's past and present economies are astrophysical extensions of an economic wealth system transplanted from the heavens to the earth.

Gold is good because it is earth's store of wealth.

Gold is good because it is earth's global wealth engine.

Gold is good because God said it was good.

Towb, the Hebrew word used in Genesis 2:12 for "good," means something beautiful, pleasant, and agreeable. When God described gold as good, His intention was for us to see the beauty in it and for it to be pleasant to our senses. But most importantly, God meant for it to agree with us. God deposited this supreme and incomparable wealth mineral into the earth with a preordained plan for it to agree with us while working hand in hand with our efforts. God called it good because it is beautiful, pleasant, and agrees with us.

The Birth of the Wealth Cycle

Gold is the cradle of a wealth system, and every human who has ever lived has been somehow connected to and affected by it throughout their entire lives. Candidly, the world's entire global economy past, present, and future was financed by a heavenly bank, the currency being gold and the depositor being God. Again, gold was the beginning of God's perpetual wealth system on the earth. Therefore, gold served as a nursery for infinite amounts of wealth, a dynamo that is perpetually creating wealth for distribution and redistribution even today. Serving as both seed and stimulus for an infant global wealth system, gold became the fountainhead of all economies to come and the nursery of every system of wealth exchange.

Obviously, since gold was accepted and set forth as a store of value both public and private, it has been used as the basis for all kinds of currencies for almost as long as monetary systems have existed in the world. Since its discovery, gold has served as the motivation and measure for mankind's wealth and financial transactions. Not surprisingly, gold has also demonstrated an inherent capacity to increase in value exponentially throughout the ages. Gold has never been nor will ever be without value. No other metal possesses this unique quality to the extent gold does.

The Gold Is Good

The pulse of the world's economy is measured by the value of gold. From an economic perspective, gold is at the heart of and guarantees the value of the currencies in circulation today. It is the global gold reserves that make money worth what it is worth. For thousands of years gold has operated in societies worldwide as a medium of exchange, or money. It becomes clear the purpose of gold was God's way for installing a perpetual wealth system into the world and introducing economies into the earth. The economies of the nations of the earth are simply systems for the exchange of wealth and serve as conduits for either increase or decrease.

Since ancient times the value of gold has been recognized throughout the world. It has long served as the bedrock upon which the financial systems of the nations are built. The strength of gold is seen in its ability to appreciate in value. The resilience of gold is seen in its ability to bridge economic systems from ancient to modern times. This is true whether it is in its raw form, minted coinage, and paper or digital currency. Currently, forty percent of the consumption of gold produced in the world continues to be used for investments.

Gold, when measured out, became money. It's beauty, scarcity, and density coupled with the ease by which it could be melted, formed, and measured made it a natural medium of trade. It was gold that gave rise to the concept of money itself, its chief characteristics being it was private, portable and divisible. In time, gold was forged into standardized coins that replaced barter arrangements, making trade much easier.

The monetary standard based upon gold is what makes the world's economies possible. The concept of money allowed the earth's economies to expand and prosper because gold became the basis for a value system of exchange. All other derivatives of wealth such as global currencies, petrodollars, digital currencies, and the world's many stock market assets all trace their lineage to gold.

The earth's wealth engine had been created.

The fuel for this engine is gold.

Gold is a store of wealth.

The gold belongs to God.

Therefore, the earth's gold is where God has stored His divine wealth.

Taking Action

There is a constant temptation to see gold and wealth only as possessions. However, nothing could be further from the truth. The reality is that gold, wealth and abundance are actually tools. A hammer is a tool as well, but it can be used to either build something or to tear something apart. Likewise, wealth can be used to build a life or it can be used to tear a life apart.

The amazing qualities of gold detailed in this chapter should generate an appreciation for the mind of God. Although the physical properties of gold are quite remarkable, it's the power of gold we must come to respect. How many wars have been fought over gold? How many people have been robbed in the streets for their gold? How many governments hoard it in underground vaults in their efforts to reign supreme in the world's wealth?

Yes, gold is valuable. And, yes, it is powerful. But never forget it is a tool. It is the method by which God deposited wealth into the earth. Wealth is the ultimate hammer, and should be used to build some great things for God!

It goes without saying that the wealth system on the earth is not something that should intimidate you. Not a day passes that we don't hear about billion-dollar companies or trillion-dollar deficits. With so much money constantly flowing here and there, it can become quite daunting when it comes to the thought of jumping into the tidal wave of wealth.

But always remember that wealth is God's invention.

Prosperity, abundance, and increase aren't things we should become jaded about, but rather blessings we should become educated about. Take the necessary time to educate yourself about how wealth works. There are numerous great resources available to help educate you about how wealth works. The internet is another powerful tool and depository of information.

Make the knowledge of wealth an important part of your intellectual and spiritual pursuits.

4

WEALTH CREATION

In the beginning God created the heavens and the earth.

Genesis 1:1

As the sovereign Creator of the universe, God is the architect of all wealth, prosperity, abundance, and increase. When God created the heavens and the earth, wealth was a fundamental and important part of that design. And since God is a Spirit, the remarkable concepts of wealth, prosperity, abundance, and increase are spiritual as well.

Wealth is spiritual.

Wealth is ancient.

Wealth is divine.

Wealth is supernatural.

Wealth envelops the planet, exists in abundance, and has richly influenced every continent. Coursing through the economies of every inhabited nation, the planet's enormous wealth reserve has helped to shape and transform the countries and cities of the world, and it will continue to do so in the ages to come. It can be seen in the abundance of riches contained within the borders of every country. It has impacted every human being who has lived before us and will continue to impact every person who is yet to come.

The sheer amount of wealth amassed upon the earth is absolutely staggering. Conservatively, the planet's worth has been estimated to be nearly five quadrillion dollars ($5,000,000,000,000,000). While this calculation might seem mind-boggling, the actual value is most likely much higher. The majority of economists believe there is no way to accurately determine the tremendous value of the earth's resources and, in that particular sense, the planet would be considered priceless. What is evident, however, is the earth is a world filled with wealth.

As the Creator of wealth, God determined exactly how wealth should and would work. Subsequently, fixed laws have governed the productive and successful flow of wealth for thousands of years. There are many techniques, strategies, processes and procedures used for coordinating the flow of wealth around the world, and because these methodologies are established and unchanging, they can be both learned and mastered.

Conceived in the mind of God, the planet's wealth system is engineered to be powerful, prosperous, perpetual and predictable. Every financial system known to mankind must obey the precise and predetermined economic laws established by God. And to the spiritually discerning, it becomes clear the wealth system of earth was designed and purposed to be a functioning extension of the wealth system of heaven.

With these thoughts in mind, an enlightened Christian understands that only the Bible can successfully teach us to both navigate and wield such an immense and powerful commodity as wealth. Since wealth can be as unfathomably beneficial as it can be devastatingly destructive, its study must be approached by equal amounts of humility and conviction.

Ultimately, the examination of wealth must be the search for truth, and the Word of God must be the final authority on the topic. Only the Bible can grant the revelation and illumination needed to properly comprehend the divine nature, origin, and purpose of wealth. Only the Bible contains the knowledge necessary to educate Christians regarding the marvelous ways wealth is beneficial to them. It was the Apostle Paul's earnest prayer that all Christians might experience this type of enlightenment:

I pray that the eyes of your heart may be enlightened, so that you will know what is the hope of His calling, what are the riches of the glory of His inheritance in the saints.

Ephesians 1:18

The Bible is clear that every born-again Christian has been supplied with a vast inheritance granted to them by way of the redemptive work of Jesus Christ. This divine inheritance has ample provisions for spirit, soul, and body. We have a Heavenly Father Who holds the universe in His hands and He desires to shower His children with blessings and increase. Every Christian has an inheritance as a child of God. Furthermore, this inheritance has been guaranteed by the promises of God, an inheritance that guarantees you both material and financial prosperity while living upon this earth.

Whether or not the full potential of that inheritance is realized, however, is dependent on each respective individual. My personal experience in observing why some people fail while others succeed can be summed up in these two conclusions: People are defeated by their own self-imposed limitations, or they are defeated because they have become imprisoned by society, situations, circumstances, or erroneous teaching. As a result, the great majority of Christians never become all they could or should be.

As I mentioned, everything we need to know about wealth can be found in the Bible. Only the Bible can develop the "God-mindedness" an individual needs to ensure the proper motives for wealth creation and accumulation. Additionally, a proper biblical mindset is needed as a defense strong enough to stand against the twin temptations of covetousness and greed. It is supremely important every Christian receive wisdom and divine insight from the Scriptures when approaching the topics of wealth, prosperity, abundance, and increase. Only the Bible can teach us how to wield such a powerful tool as wealth.

Wealth, Prosperity, Abundance, and Increase

Carefully consider the following seven passages of Scripture:

> **But thou shalt remember the LORD thy God: for it is he that giveth thee power to get wealth, that he may establish his covenant which he sware unto thy fathers, as it is this day.**
>
> **Deuteronomy 8:18 (KJV)**

> **If they hear and serve Him,**
> **They will end their days in prosperity**
> **And their years in pleasures.**
>
> **Job 36:11**

> **Praise the LORD!**
> **How blessed is the man who fears the LORD,**
> **Who greatly delights in His commandments.**
> **His descendants will be mighty on earth;**
> **The generation of the upright will be blessed.**

> **Wealth and riches are in his house,**
>> **And his righteousness endures forever.**
>
>> **Psalm 112:1–3**

> **Adversity pursues sinners,**
>> **But the righteous will be rewarded with prosperity.**
>
>> **Proverbs 13:21**

> Give, and it will be given to you. They will pour into your lap a good measure—pressed down, shaken together, and running over. For by your standard of measure it will be measured to you in return.
>
>> **Luke 6:38**

> **And my God will supply all your needs according to His riches in glory in Christ Jesus.**
>
>> **Philippians 4:19**

> Now He who supplies seed to the sower and bread for food will supply and multiply your seed for sowing and increase the harvest of your righteousness; you will be enriched in everything for all liberality, which through us is producing thanksgiving to God.
>
>> **2 Corinthians 9:10–11**

A Polarizing Topic

The above verses vividly demonstrate how God has given His people the means to create, acquire, and receive wealth. It is important to note the fulfillment of the above verses are conditional upon a number of crucial commands such as obedience, honoring and serving God, living a holy and righteous life, and demonstrating generosity in giving.

The obvious question then becomes, "If these promises are true, why do so many Christians struggle financially?"

It stands to reason if there is a supernatural power at work for the acquisition of wealth – which, according to the above Bible references, there is — there must also be a supernatural power at work for the loss of wealth, which, according to the Bible, there is as well. The glaring fact that so many Christians struggle with poverty and lack while living in the bright light of God's promises is proof there is an unseen and powerful force actively warring against their biblical promise of wealth.

There are a plethora of other passages throughout the Bible that address the topics of wealth, prosperity, abundance, and increase. Sadly, these verses only serve to offend and anger many Christians. But they are promises rooted in the Scripture, and they are true nonetheless. Because the concepts of wealth have been equally championed and condemned by Christians throughout the years, there is no shortage of positions and opinions that have resulted in much confusion on the topic.

Biblical wealth has become a controversial subject as the result of conflicting viewpoints from so many people, saved and unsaved alike. This is especially true regarding the importance of wealth along with its impact on everyday life. However, we are not interested in what others have to say about wealth; we are interested in what God has to say about it. Prosperity, abundance, increase, riches, harvest, treasure, possessions, and blessings are all words connected to wealth, words which are found hundreds of times throughout the Bible.

Wealth is not a bad word. Indeed, it is a Bible word. It is a covenant word that God uses frequently in both the Old and New Testaments. The correct biblical frame of reference for wealth's distribution is that God is the source of all good gifts.

Every good thing given and every perfect gift is from above, coming down from the Father.

James 1:17

Tragically, many critics believe wealth is not God's will for His children. Christians are taught that they should condemn wealth and that material possessions, money, and abundance should be shunned. However, that is not the mindset of God nor is it supported by the examples found throughout His Word.

Now, take a moment to reflect on what is recorded in John 10:10:

The thief cometh not, but for to steal, and to kill, and to destroy: I am come that they might have life, and that they might have it more abundantly.

John 10:10 (KJV)

John 10:10 describes God as a giver and Satan as a thief. Even as God is continuously creating and giving to His children, Satan is continuously destroying and stealing from those very people. As a result, an unceasing battle has raged for centuries between the Church and the secular world over the wealth of the earth. This endless war for wealth has resulted in countless economic casualties amongst the sons and daughters of God. The unabated theft and ongoing destruction of their wealth has had a concurrent effect on the Church's ability to do more in the world. The inheritances of far too many Christians go undefended and their covenant rights unrealized.

A New Direction

I believe we can address these devastating trends, reverse course, and begin God's people on the journey toward the fulfillment of 3 John 2:

> **Beloved, I pray that in all respects you may prosper and be in good health, just as your soul prospers.**
>
> **3 John 2**

One of the most enlightening verses in the New Testament showcasing God's will toward prosperity is 3 John 2. This verse plainly states that prosperity is God's will for His people. Prospering means flourishing and growing in wealth. According to the Bible, the prayer of the Apostle John was that God's people would prosper in proportion to the prosperity of their health and soul.

Regarding the words of John, *The Pulpit Commentary* says, "The apostle wishes that his earthly career may be as bright as his spiritual career is, may he have a sound body for his sound mind, and may his fortunes be sound also. The Greek word for 'prosper' means to 'have a good career.'" Those who would condemn the prosperity of Christians would do well to heed the words of John. A prosperous Christian is one who has learned how to continuously reap of the earth's wealth.

While it is visibly true there has been much abuse in the church with respect to prosperity, this abuse in no way invalidates God's promises concerning biblical wealth. Truth is truth and does not cease to be true even when error abounds. We should never be satisfied with anything less than God's perfect will for us when it comes to wealth, prosperity, abundance, and increase.

The New Testament believer must choose to believe and receive wealth as both an important part of their inheritance and a necessary part of what God is doing in His church today. Faith is essential to the believer who desires to experience the fullness of their inheritance:

And without faith it is impossible to please Him, for he who comes to God must believe that He is and that He is a rewarder of those who seek Him.

Hebrews 11:6

God is good.

God is a giver.

God is a rewarder.

There is a wealth system on the earth, a system that God created and utilizes to bless His people through wealth, prosperity, abundance, and increase. It is our responsibility to educate ourselves about this wealth system, along with how to access it, navigate it, and ultimately benefit from it. Ongoing ignorance, either intentional or unintentional, will only lead to the increase of poverty and lack.

My people are destroyed for lack of knowledge.

Hosea 4:6

Following the need for salvation, the infilling of the Holy Spirit, and the process of maturing spiritually, one of a Christian's most pressing needs is to walk in the realities of biblical wealth. This is a bold statement, but it is one born from decades of personal observation and interaction with God's people. If there is an Achilles' Heel in the church it is the constant, crippling and universal lack of wealth from which the majority of its members suffer. The failure to prosper is a noticeable weakness in the Body of Christ, an obvious deficiency to which many have turned a blind eye. As a result, financial struggles and hardships afflict Christians throughout the greater part of their lives.

But this is not the type of life God intended for His people.

A thoughtful study of the Bible reveals biblical wealth is a sacred thing between God and His people. This is a powerful, life-altering truth and reality of the New Covenant. And if biblical wealth is sacred, it stands to reason the path to biblical wealth would be sacred as well.

Much of what has been written regarding biblical wealth is informational, and rightly so, but there is more beyond that which is revelatory as well. One of the reasons many live in the shallows regarding wealth is because the prevalent teachings on the topic are strictly informational; letters with no life. In contrast to that, it is revelation that leads to inspiration. And inspiration is so powerful because it results in change! What good are a thousand books written about biblical wealth if they don't result in change?

God's people yearn to be transformed from a life of poverty and lack into one of prosperity and abundance. It has been my observation that many Christians are eager to receive a deeper, yet balanced, revelation on the subject of biblical wealth. The principles found in the Word of God will show people how the transfer of wealth works, when it works, why it works, and whom it will work for. Furthermore, the Bible dramatically demonstrates the supernatural dynamics of biblical wealth transference and allocation. This knowledge will strengthen, position, and empower God's people as it did the patriarchs memorialized throughout the Bible.

God established the earth with a vast and perpetual wealth system. This system has worked successfully for thousands of years and is designed to work for each and every Christian today. Christians should be neither ashamed nor embarrassed to experience prosperity. The laws of biblical wealth have not lost their vitality and are encapsulated in promises waiting to be discovered, explored, and activated so God's people can experience life more abundantly.

Taking Action

As your mind and heart begin to expand and take in the vast possibilities of God's incredible and powerful wealth system, you will undoubtedly discover the need to change course in a number of areas.

Walking in the realities of biblical wealth is largely a result of parting ways with the realities of secular poverty. A poverty mindset is a belief system that life is full of scarcity. It is the thinking that things are hard to get and hard to earn. Those with this mindset refuse to invest in themselves because they don't want to spend money or exert the necessary effort.

If you want to change the direction of your life, then you will need to change the signs you are following. Are you allowing the world to determine what success looks like for you? Or are you allowing the Bible to determine what success looks like for you? These are hard questions we all must answer while on our respective journeys.

When you are reading the Bible, try to be more aware of how wealth and prosperity scriptures apply to you and your specific circumstance. Everyone is unique in God's eyes and none of us are replicas of one another. What works for someone else might not necessarily work for you. However, when you discover the particular avenue God intends to bless *you* with, it will be like catching lightning in a bottle!

5

WEALTH IS A CROWN

A crown is a form of headwear that represents power, triumph, and victory. Indicative of royal authority, it is the emblem of a government or kingdom. A crown is also the honor or reward bestowed upon those who have been distinguished by a great achievement, promotion, or victory.

According to *Baker's Evangelical Dictionary of Biblical Theology*, the placement of a crown on a person's head was the symbolic act that the individual was henceforth set apart for a special task or calling. A crowning was a ceremony that demonstrated the consecrated role of the wearer and reflected his or her exalted position. In the Old Testament, a crown indicated the presence of honor, especially as a person entered into a special position. The Hebrew word for *crown* is *atar*, which means to encircle or surround. This was a word used during warfare to describe either offensive or defensive strategies, depending on the situation.

In the New Testament, the definition of a crown is further expanded upon and refers to the victory garland presented at the winning of a race. Crowns were bestowed in regal coronations and many times worn into battle. It was a common practice for winners, champions, and conquerors to wear physical crowns. Kings and queens have worn crowns since antiquity and, as a result, have been the recipients of great honor and responsibility throughout the ages.

The Crowns Christians Wear

The Bible teaches that born-again Christians have been crowned with numerous crowns. Peter described one such crown in 1 Peter 5:4 as an "unfading crown of glory." The Apostle Paul refers to a "crown of righteousness" in 2 Timothy 4:8 and a "crown of rejoicing" in 1 Thessalonians 2:19 (NKJV). Most importantly, the "crown of life" is mentioned in both James 1:12 and Revelation 2:10.

All of these crowns come from God, and He is the One who has crowned us. In Revelation 19:12, Jesus stands as the King "who is crowned with many crowns." In all of these examples, the imagery conveyed is that of honor, rule, sovereignty, authority and power. These crowns, and the authority of the One backing these crowns, impact and influence everything in the life of a Christian.

We should not be surprised God has designated us as royalty. Royalty is the result of relationship, and as a member of God's royal family, you have been given all the rights and responsibilities that come with that relationship and position.

> **But you are A CHOSEN RACE, A royal PRIESTHOOD, A HOLY NATION, A PEOPLE FOR God's OWN POSSESSION, so that you may proclaim the excellencies of Him who has called you out of darkness into His marvelous light.**
>
> **1 Peter 2:9**

Wealth Is a Crown

Christians hold royal positions, and those in royal positions wear crowns. Of course, we understand these crowns to be figurative in nature, just as the sword of the spirit and the shield of faith are figurative. Metaphors are figures of speech used throughout scripture to represent or symbolize something else, bringing attention to similarities between the two ideas. The sword of the Spirit is the Word of God, with which we use to fight. The shield of faith is our belief system, which offers us protection. The crowns of God are specific redemptive realities for the various spheres of life the Lord has granted us authority within.

Proverbs 14:24 describes another powerful and important crown:

> **Wealth is a crown for the wise.**
>
> **Proverbs 14:24 (NLT)**

For the child of God, wealth is a crown just as glory, righteousness, rejoicing, and life are crowns. Correspondingly, the crown of wealth also indicates a position of power, triumph, and victory. It also refers to a life of wealth emblematic of royal authority. In Proverbs 14:24, the exact same Hebrew word for crown (*atar*) is used. The intent is that wealth, in like manner, was to encircle the righteous. In the life of a Christian, wealth can be used for both offensive and defensive purposes.

THE CROWNING OF DAVID

In 2 Samuel 5, the Bible records the events surrounding the coronation of David as he was anointed King over Israel:

> **Then all the tribes of Israel came to David at Hebron and said, "Behold, we are your bone and your flesh. Previously, when Saul was king over us, you were the one who led Israel out and in. And the LORD said to you, 'You will shepherd**

> **My people Israel, and you will be a ruler over Israel.'" So all the elders of Israel came to the king at Hebron, and King David made a covenant with them before the LORD at Hebron; then they anointed David king over Israel.**
>
>

2 Samuel 5:1–3

The crowning of King David at the ancient city of Hebron produced two powerful, yet very opposite, results in the land: transformation and confrontation. The highlight of this revolutionary change of authority came when David and his army captured Zion, the place that would be Israel's center of worship. The victory that had been impossible for Israel throughout their whole history became possible when David was crowned king. David was a servant king with a shepherd's heart, and when Israel bowed its knee to King David, the nation was transformed, and the kingdom expanded. The crown, and the authority of the One backing the crown, changed everything.

But even as David's coronation produced transformation, it also led to fierce confrontation. The Philistines, an aggressive and warmongering people known for their continuous conflicts with the Israelites, felt threatened and became enraged at Israel's transformation under the leadership of their newly crowned king.

In David's day, the Philistines occupied the region of Philistia, an area located on the southwest corner of Palestine. This territory on the south Mediterranean coast of Israel was also known as the land of the Philistines. The Hebrew word, *Philistia,* means "to linger in grief and mourning," a defeatist attitude that manifests through those who deplore, bemoan and regret the success of others. There could not have been a better description of the Philistines who were an angry, jealous, and bitter people that exhibited constant opposition to anything God was doing.

When the Philistines heard that David had been crowned king over Israel and saw the transformation that came as a result, they challenged him to battle on two different occasions in the Valley of Rephaim. With both challenges, David requested wisdom from the Lord, and each time the Lord directed and led David to strike down and defeat the armies of the Philistines. David's coronation resulted in confrontation, yet the King did not hesitate for one second to defend his crown.

The Promise of Confrontation

Even as David's coronation into kingship provoked confrontation, your coronation into wealth will provoke confrontation as well. We have all witnessed the countless negative and vicious barbs hurled at any Christian who dares to embrace the promise of biblical wealth. Clearly, those who champion biblical wealth are emphatically for it while those who reject biblical wealth are emphatically against it.

As a Christian, you should expect these hostile ambushes from modern-day financial philistines. Today's philistines are those who disdain sound biblical doctrine and values. They are those who are uninformed in special areas of knowledge and refuse to exert any effort to become better or even consider change. They are those who are in constant conflict with Christians and cannot rest until they have marginalized and dismissed every financial benefit contained in the New Covenant. They will challenge your crown again and again, enticing you onto the battlefield, all because of the position you occupy. But like David, Christians should not hesitate for one second to defend their crowns.

It is relatively easy to identify modern-day financial philistines. They are those who express their strong disapproval of biblical wealth. They abhor and are offended by the topics of prosperity, abundance, and increase. They are those who wallow in mourning when a Christian experiences the promise of wealth. They bitterly demonstrate their opposition as evidenced by their hate of the prosperity of others.

Financial philistines deplore the prosperity of others.

They bewail the prosperity of others.

They bemoan the prosperity of others.

They rue the prosperity of others.

They regret the prosperity of others.

A Distorted Understanding of Wealth

Financial philistines are emphatic that God's Word condemns the accumulation of wealth. They cite familiar passages from the Bible such as, "Blessed are the poor" (Luke 6:20) and, "It is easier for a camel to go through the eye of a needle than for a rich man to enter the kingdom of heaven" (Luke 18:25). They boldly declare the virtues of poverty while denouncing the vices of wealth.

However, these scriptures must be taken together with others that present wealth in a different and balanced perspective. Wealth was the natural result of hard work and diligence and was recognized as a blessing from God to be enjoyed:

> **Poor is he who works with a negligent hand,**
> **But the hand of the diligent makes rich.**
> **He who gathers in summer is a son who acts wisely,**
> **But he who sleeps in harvest is a son who acts shamefully.**
>
> **Proverbs 10:4–5**

> **Here is what I have seen to be good and fitting: to eat, to drink and enjoy oneself in all one's labor in which he toils**

under the sun during the few years of his life which God has given him; for this is his reward. Furthermore, as for every man to whom God has given riches and wealth, He has also empowered him to eat from them and to receive his reward and rejoice in his labor; this is the gift of God. For he will not often consider the years of his life, because God keeps him occupied with the gladness of his heart.

Ecclesiastes 5:18–20

In the New Testament, Christians are further counseled to keep wealth in its proper perspective. This entails the understanding that God gives liberally to His children for their enjoyment. Yet, at the same time, He warns us to not place our trust in the very wealth He has so generously supplied. The love of wealth coupled with the desire to become wealthy carry with them the dangerous potential to destroy an individual's life:

But those who want to get rich fall into temptation and a snare and many foolish and harmful desires which plunge men into ruin and destruction. For the love of money is a root of all sorts of evil, and some by longing for it have wandered away from the faith and pierced themselves with many griefs.

1 Timothy 6:9–10

If I have put my confidence in gold,
   And called fine gold my trust,
If I have gloated because my wealth was great,
   And because my hand had secured so much;
If I have looked at the sun when it shone
   Or the moon going in splendor,
And my heart became secretly enticed,
   And my hand threw a kiss from my mouth,

> **That too would have been an iniquity calling for judgment,
> For I would have denied God above.**
>
> **Job 31:24–28**

While it is true the Bible distinguishes between the possession of wealth and the love of wealth, it is the love of wealth that is steadfastly condemned, *not* the possession of wealth. Contrariwise, it is selfishness, greed, and the hoarding of wealth that is disdained by the Lord. God is greatly grieved when the wealthy become oblivious to the cries of the poor and less fortunate.

Wealth is not the problem.

The possession of wealth is not the problem.

The accumulation of wealth is not the problem.

The greed and covetousness of mankind is the problem.

PROSPERITY UNDER ATTACK

It's no secret the secular world holds a dangerous and toxic viewpoint of wealth when it relates to Christians, ministers, and the church. It is a common belief throughout much of the earth that the church, its ministers, and its Christians should have little or nothing to do with wealth. Sadly, this is a position that has been adopted by countless ministers and even Christians as well. Many good-hearted and well-intentioned ministers have been labeled as prosperity preachers who are peddling a prosperity gospel, and a quick search of the internet produces millions of slanderous results. This secular stance flies in the face of established Scripture and the experiences of numerous men and women of God found in the Bible.

Satan has declared a war on prosperity. Why do Christians offer such little resistance to the enemy's siege? Why do so many valiantly resist the devil in other areas of their Christianity yet exhibit such indifference to poverty and lack? Have you ever wondered why Christians celebrate the time when Jesus turned worthless water into valuable wine yet refuse to believe for that same transformative miracle in their finances? Have you asked yourself why Christians don't exercise economic faith to feed their families, yet they joyfully recount the time Jesus multiplied the bread and fish to feed the thousands? It is this type of double-mindedness and doubt that paralyzes the financial advancement of God's people.

Adding to that, when will God's children stop listening to a lost world that is dictating what they can and cannot have? The secular world is drunk with wealth, yet their opposition to the church possessing even a fraction of that same wealth is legendary.

There is a striking double standard when it comes to this world's wealth and resources. Some of the most vicious opponents are those in various religious orders. Yet these are those who faithfully support manmade denominations that possess hundreds of millions of dollars. Among many denominations, wealth is a taboo subject, quickly condemned, while those who demonstrate the faith to prosper are quickly labeled greedy sinners and dismissed as just the same. It is high time for Christians to look to the Bible for guidance and stop letting others set wealth standards for their lives.

Even in the light of Scripture, the attacks against a Christian's covenant rights to wealth continue to intensify. That dimension of a Christian's inheritance is mercilessly mocked, shunned, shamed, ridiculed, and belittled. Among the ranks of the secular mainstream media, biblical prosperity has become the source of countless jokes, sarcasm, rancor, and disparaging insults. Ministers who advocate wealth by promoting the promise and power of biblical wealth will continue to be denigrated, derided, and disdained. Much energy has been expended into the crusade of denying Christians what God has promised them.

The secular world has imposed their economic expectations upon you. And since Satan is the god of this world, the reality is these expectations are his subtle limitations and silent restrictions that come in dangerous disguise. These expectations tell you how much you should earn, what your net worth should be, and how much money should be in your bank accounts. These expectations, limitations, and restrictions are incredibly hazardous because they are the unspoken economic rules that the majority of the world's population obeys without question.

Satan would love to halt your forward progress and bar you from the best God has provided for you. When you make the decision to break out of the secular world's economic cage, your mind becomes free to take in everything God has promised for you.

The harsh truth is that Satan has weaponized God's promises against His own people. But now, it is time to launch a war on poverty.

THE TRANSFORMATIVE POWER OF WEALTH

David's coronation also ushered in a season of transformation, victory and expansion. Your coronation will usher in the same. In order to fully appreciate the crown of wealth, an individual must first understand the biblical purpose and power of wealth. Several commentaries help provide valuable insight.

Regarding Proverbs 14:24, *Matthew Poole's Commentary* states, "The crown of the wise is their riches. They are a singular advantage and ornament to them, partly as they make their wisdom more regarded, when the poor man's wisdom is despised, and partly as they give a man great opportunity to discover and exercise his wisdom or virtue by laying out his riches to the honor and service of God and to the great and manifold good of the world, which also highly tends to his own glory and happiness."

Gill's Exposition of the Entire Bible says, "The crown of the wise is their riches being used by them to increase and improve their knowledge and wisdom, and for the good of men, are an honor to them, and give them credit and reputation among men of sense and goodness."

"Riches are an ornament to a wise man," adds *The Pulpit Commentary*. "They enhance and set off his wisdom in the eyes of others, enable him to use it to advantage, and are not the snare which they might be because they are employed religiously and profitably for the good of others."

In *A Commentary on the Holy Scriptures*, author Johann Lange says, "The well-earned possessions of the wise become his honor, are a real adornment to him, for which he is with good reason praised." Building upon this thought, *Ellicott's Bible Commentary for English Readers* states that the wealth of the wise displays their wisdom, and brings it "more prominently into notice."

About the crown, William Kelly's *Major Works* commentary says, "The crown, not of the foolish, but of the wise, is their riches, for these turn their wealth to the account of unselfish goodness and the relief of human misery, and the furtherance of God's will and glory. They would be rich toward God."

"The idea is," wrote D. Thomas in *The Biblical Illustrator*, "that a wise man would so use his wealth that it will become a crown to him. By using it to promote his own mental and spiritual cultivation, and to ameliorate the woes and to augment the happiness of the world, his wealth gives him a diadem more lustrous by far than all the diamond crowns of kings."

LET NO ONE TAKE YOUR CROWN

These commentators and expositors understood the true purpose and power of wealth. They also understood the dangers connected to forfeiting that crown. Those who relinquish their crowns of wealth, either willingly or unwillingly, usually do so as the result of attacks, ignorance, and erroneous teaching. So serious was the threat that Jesus Christ personally addressed the danger of doing so in Revelation 3:11:

I am coming soon. Hold fast what you have, so that no one may seize your crown.

Revelation 3:11 (ESV)

The removal of a crown always results in ruin and shame. When a person is stripped of their crown, it is a humiliating event that leaves them exposed and disgraced. Every time a Christian rejects, forsakes, or renounces the Bible's promises of wealth, he or she has removed their crown of wealth. This decision inevitably leads to financial ruin and shame. Many Christians hastily discard their crowns of wealth while eagerly clothing themselves in rags of poverty. This should not be the case with the sons and daughters of God.

Look to yourselves (take care) that you may not lose (throw away or destroy) all that we *and* you have labored for, but that you may [persevere until you] win *and* receive back a perfect reward [in full].

2 John 8 (AMPC)

You must not *lose* your crown.

You must not *throw away* your crown.

You must not *destroy* your crown.

You must commit to receiving and achieving victory in every area of your life, which includes the promise of biblical wealth as well. You cannot afford to part with your wealth, prosperity, abundance, and increase on any terms.

The Crown of Wealth is priceless.

The Crown of Wealth is powerful.

The Crown of Wealth is life changing.

It is precious beyond description, more valuable than the world's most costly gems! Wealth, prosperity, abundance, and increase are blessings that are as real as God's Word. These benefits of a Christian's inheritance should be diligently sought out so that they might be experienced in the lives of God's people. These promises – along with their fulfillment — should find their place in the royal treasury of every single son and daughter of God.

TAKING ACTION

If wealth is a crown, then you might be asking yourself, "Where in the world is *my* crown?"

Don't worry.

Simply because you haven't been aware of something, possibly for your entire life, doesn't mean it isn't there. When David was just a shepherd boy and long before he became a king, he most likely had no idea of the riches he would come to possess later in life. But his crown was still there. When God sent the prophet Samuel to anoint the next king of Israel, He said, "Do not look at his appearance or the height of his stature, for God sees not as a man sees. Man looks at the outward appearance, but the Lord looks at the heart." The crown on your *head* starts with the crown in your *heart*.

David encountered two very different types of people on his way to the throne: those who would come to celebrate him and those who would come to attack him. Ask yourself these questions: When a blessing comes into your life, who celebrates with you? Who attacks you? The answers to these questions will give you a pretty good idea of those who desire to see you rise to the top and others who may desire to see you drop to the bottom.

As a result of prosperity being largely under attack today, you will need to not only fortify your position by surrounding yourself with people of like faith, you will also need to launch your own assault on poverty. This means becoming much more disciplined in the financial realm of life. It means taking on less debt as well as attacking and paying down the existing debt you carry. It might mean living in a smaller house for a season or driving a much older vehicle for a time.

So be patient. You are sowing the seeds of future increase, and seeds take time to germinate, take root and grow. Whatever you do, don't let any financial philistines talk you out of what God has promised to you.

6

THE STRENGTH OF WEALTH AND THE STING OF DEBT

What is wealth?

One dictionary defines wealth in terms of the value of everything a person owns. Another defines it as a sizable mass of money and other valuables. A third dictionary is a little broader in its definition and focuses on an abundant supply of valuable or desirable things.

The Bible states that God has given *you* the power to *make wealth*.

> **But you shall remember the LORD your God, for it is He who is giving you power to make wealth, that He may confirm His covenant which He swore to your fathers, as it is this day.**
>
> **Deuteronomy 8:18**

A closer analysis of a few pivotal words in Deuteronomy 8:18 brings deeper meaning to the verse. The Hebrew word for *power* also means ability. The Hebrew word for *make* also means accomplish.

Furthermore, the Hebrew word for *wealth* also means strength. Deuteronomy 8:18 literally means, *God has given you the ability to accomplish strength through wealth.*

In others words, wealth grants its possessors strength.

The Apostle Paul, in his second letter to the Corinthian church, summed up the many characteristics of wealth in a singular verse:

And God is able to bestow every blessing on you in abundance, so that richly enjoying all sufficiency at all times, you may have ample means for all good works.

2 Corinthians 9:8 (WNT)

To a Christian, wealth is much more than just having a bunch of stuff. True biblical wealth is experiencing a complete sufficiency in any situation, for every need, at all times. Sufficiency is defined as having enough of something to achieve a purpose or to fulfill a need. It is strategic wealth, or wealth with a purpose. God's wealth system makes His people strong because of the ever-present sufficiency it provides.

Not only are you promised to richly enjoy sufficiency at all times, but there will be more than enough to be a blessing to others as well. Indeed, this was the blessing promised to Abraham:

And I will make you a great nation, And I will bless you, and make your name great; And so you shall be a blessing.

Genesis 12:2

WEALTH CONSISTS OF MATERIAL POSSESSIONS

The Bible is a book of wealth which records many examples of those blessed with spectacular material riches. The stories and accounts of these individuals are interwoven with the promises, principles, and procedures essential for understanding and receiving prosperity. Throughout the centuries, theologians have extensively studied and examined the great wealth of the patriarchs. Abraham, Isaac, Jacob, Joseph, Job, David, and Solomon are all examples of those who commanded vast amounts of riches and wealth. These scriptural examples of faith never shied away from their abundance and never offered up excuses for their increase, rather they offered instead only praise and thanksgiving to God. They understood God's supernatural wealth system, and were unapologetic about their prosperity.

These men were rich in gold, land, and possessions. The material assets held by these leaders are comparable to being owners of modern, billion-dollar businesses. Amazingly, as they continued to profess their faith and allegiance to God, their possessions became even greater. During times of plight or famine, these men didn't suffer, but instead, continued to enjoy ever-increasing, prosperous lives. Even in adverse times and difficult circumstances, they continued to receive material blessings in whatever far off lands their travels would take them, with their great wealth making them the envy of surrounding nations. Their unflinching loyalty to God was rewarded with ever-increasing riches and wealth. Many of these individuals were blessed with such strong economic and business wisdom they continued to impact their lineage and countries long after their deaths.

Wealth, prosperity, abundance, and increase have demonstrated a divine connection to God throughout the Bible. The Old and New Testaments both clearly reveal the heart of God pertaining to this important subject. There are many unchanging qualities and characteristics that are inherent to wealth, and if more Christians understood the power of it, they would spend less time condemning it and more time embracing it.

Please bear with me patiently and thoughtfully as you consider the extensive truths regarding biblical wealth that follow.

God Delights in Prosperity

Let them shout for joy and rejoice, who favor my vindication;
And let them say continually, "The LORD be magnified, Who delights in the prosperity of His servant."

Psalm 35:27

Prosperity is the state of being wealthy or having a rich and full life. It is a condition in which a person is flourishing, thriving, and doing well financially.

Barnes' Notes on the Whole Bible says, "Let the Lord be magnified — Be regarded as great, exalted, glorious. Let the effect be to elevate their conceptions of the character of God by the fact that he has thus interposed in a righteous cause, and has shown that he is the friend of the wronged and the oppressed. Which hath pleasure in the prosperity of his servant — Who delights to make his friends prosperous and happy — let them see that this is the character of God, and let them thus be led to rejoice in him evermore."

Wealth Is a Blessing

Praise the LORD!
How blessed is the man who fears the LORD,
Who greatly delights in His commandments.
His descendants will be mighty on earth;
The generation of the upright will be blessed.
Wealth and riches are in his house,

And his righteousness endures forever.

Psalm 112:1–3

A blessing is defined as God's favor and protection.

"Wealth and riches shall be in his house, in his family," records *Gill's Exposition of the Entire Bible*. "If not possessed by him, yet by his posterity. He is not hurt by his temporal riches, as others are, the prodigal, the covetous, and formal professor; he continues the good and righteous man he was, notwithstanding his riches."

The *Geneva Bible* states, "Wealth and riches shall be in his house. The godly will have abundance and contentment, because their heart is satisfied in God alone." In the *Cambridge Bible for Schools and Colleges*, it says: "The unbroken prosperity of the godly is the verdict of approval which God pronounces upon his character and conduct."

Wealth without Sorrow

**It is the blessing of the LORD that makes rich,
And He adds no sorrow to it.**

Proverbs 10:22

The "sorrow" referenced here is the deep, great sadness caused by loss, regret, or failure. God does not want the wealth of his children to be connected to suffering or pain.

Regarding wealth, *Matthew Poole's Commentary* states, "He addeth no sorrow with it, with that blessing which gives riches, but gives them content and comfort in their riches, which is a singular gift and blessing of God."

The Benson Commentary says, "Riches are not gotten merely by wisdom or diligence, but also, and especially, by God's favor and blessing."

"No sorrow goes along with the blessing," records *Gill's Exposition of the Entire Bible*, "but what is a blessing itself, as one observes; riches enjoyed through the blessing of God are not attended with that sorrow in getting, keeping, and losing them, as the riches of wicked men unlawfully gotten are. For as the good man comes by them easily, without any anxious care and sinful solicitude, he seeking the kingdom of God and his righteousness, all these things are added to him, over and above, without much thought about them, or expectation of them; so it is with great delight, pleasure, and cheerfulness, he enjoys them, and readily communicates them to others."

WEALTH BRINGS PROSPERITY AND PLEASURE

If they hear and serve Him,
    They will end their days in prosperity
And their years in pleasures.

Job 36:11

Pleasure is the feelings of joy and happiness that accompany satisfaction and enjoyment. It is the joy that accompanies getting something good or much wanted, and the condition of being pleased.

The Benson Commentary observes, "If they obey God's admonition and command, they shall spend their days in prosperity. They shall be restored to their former prosperity, and shall live and die in it abounding in worldly comforts, and delighting themselves in the love and favor of God thereby manifested to them."

Furthermore, *Gill's Exposition of the Entire Bible* says, "They shall spend their days in prosperity and their years in pleasures, which intimates, that those to whom afflictions are sanctified, and they obedient under them, when recovered out of them shall enjoy long life; not only live many days, but years, and those in great prosperity and pleasure be blessed with much temporal prosperity, which lies in riches and wealth."

Wealth Is a Fortress

**The rich man's wealth is his fortress,
The ruin of the poor is their poverty.**

Proverbs 10:15

A fortress is a strong, secured location. From its original sense of *stronghold*, it gives the image of "a large strong building or a well-protected place."

"What a fortified city is to persons in time of war, that is a rich man's wealth to him. By it he can defend himself from the injuries of others and support himself and family in times of public calamity," states *Gill's Exposition of the Entire Bible*. "Money is a defense and answers all things. The destruction of the poor is their poverty, or their poverty is their consternation, as the word signifies. It frightens them. They, knowing their circumstances, are afraid of everybody and of everything, not being able to defend themselves against their enemies or support themselves in times of public calamity, as war, famine, or pestilence."

From *Ellicott's Commentary for English Readers*: "The rich man's wealth gives him the consciousness of power, courage: whereas poverty drags a man down, and prevents his advance in life, or makes him timid, and unable to defend himself."

Barnes' Notes on the Whole Bible records, "Wealth secures its possessors against many dangers; poverty exposes men to worse evils than itself, meanness, servility, and cowardice."

WEALTH IS PROTECTION

**Wisdom along with an inheritance is good
   And an advantage to those who see the sun.
For wisdom is protection just as money is protection,
   But the advantage of knowledge is that wisdom preserves the lives of its possessors.**

Ecclesiastes 7:11–12

The definition of "protection" is being protected or the act of protecting from something unpleasant or dangerous. "To be under the shadow of wisdom is the same as to be under the shadow of money," records the *Jamieson-Fausset-Brown Bible Commentary*.

Matthew Poole's Commentary states, "It is a defense, which in Scripture usage notes both protection and refreshment, and thus far wisdom and money agree."

Ellicott's Commentary for English Readers says, "Wisdom and riches alike confer protection. A defense. Literally, a shadow."

"Wisdom shelters as money shelters," states *The Pulpit Commentary*. "Wisdom as well as money is a shield and defense to men. The literal translation given above implies that he who has wisdom and he who has money rest under a safe protection, are secure from material evil. In this respect they are alike, and have analogous claims to man's regard."

Gill's Exposition of the Entire Bible states, "For wisdom is a defense and money is a defense, or a shadow of refreshment and protection under which men sit with pleasure and safety. A man by his wisdom, and so by his money, is able to defend himself against the injuries and oppressions of others, and especially when both meet in one and the same man."

Wealth with a Purpose

> **Now He who supplies seed to the sower and bread for food will supply and multiply your seed for sowing and increase the harvest of your righteousness; you will be enriched in everything for all liberality, which through us is producing thanksgiving to God. For the ministry of this service is not only fully supplying the needs of the saints, but is also overflowing through many thanksgivings to God. Because of the proof given by this ministry, they will glorify God for your obedience to your confession of the gospel of Christ and for the liberality of your contribution to them and to all, while they also, by prayer on your behalf, yearn for you because of the surpassing grace of God in you. Thanks be to God for His indescribable gift!**
>
> 2 Corinthians 9:10–15

The word *purpose* describes the plan behind something that is created or done — its main aim or intention, goal or determination. *Barnes' Notes on the Whole Bible* says, "In all respects your riches are conferred on you for this purpose. The design of the apostle is to state to them the true reason why wealth was bestowed. It was not for the purposes of luxury and self-gratification; not to be spent in sensual enjoyment, not for parade and display; it was that it might be distributed to others in such a way as to cause thanksgiving to God."

Gill's Exposition of the Entire Bible states, "The sense is that God was not only able to give them a sufficiency and would give them a sufficiency of temporal things, as food and raiment to their satisfaction and contentment for themselves, but a fullness, an exuberance, an over-plus also. Not for luxury and intemperance, but that having such an affluence in all the good things of life, they might at all times, and upon every occasion, exercise a bountiful disposition in relieving the poor."

"God means that the basin should be always full right up to the top of the marble edge, and that the more is drawn off from it, the more should flow into it," records *MacLaren's Expositions of Holy Scripture*. "But it is very often like the reservoirs in the hills for some great city in a drought, where great stretches of the bottom are exposed, and again, when the drought breaks, are full to the top of the retaining wall. That should not be. Our Christian life should run on the high levels."

Wealth Produces More Wealth

> **Honor the LORD from your wealth**
> **And from the first of all your produce;**
> **So your barns will be filled with plenty**
> **And your vats will overflow with new wine.**
>
> **Proverbs 3:9–10**

From *The Pulpit Commentary*: "The promise held out to encourage the devotion of one's wealth to Jehovah's service, while supplying a motive which at first sight appears selfish and questionable, is in reality a trial of faith. Few persons find it easy to realize that giving it away will increase their store. Money makes money. A man who has capital finds various means of increasing it; it grows as it is judiciously employed. Thus the grace of God, duly stirred up and exercised, receives continual accession. The Christian's spiritual forces are developed by being properly directed. Providence puts in his way added opportunities, and as he uses these he is more and more strengthened and replenished."

The *Geneva Bible* states, "For the faithful distributor God gives in greater abundance."

Debt Is Not Wealth

It would be irresponsible to extol the virtues of wealth without addressing the topic of debt. Debt subjugates the borrower to the lender by way of something — typically money — that is owed or due with interest.

> **The rich rules over the poor,**
> **And the borrower becomes the lender's slave.**
>
> **Proverbs 22:7**

Wealth accumulation cannot be accomplished alongside debt accumulation. They are polar opposites and both contain the power to negate one another. The one you choose to feed is the one that will grow. Not surprisingly, the Bible contains some rather direct statements about debt:

> **Owe nothing to anyone except to love one another; for he who loves his neighbor has fulfilled the law.**
>
> **Romans 13:8**

> **The LORD will open for you His good storehouse, the heavens, to give rain to your land in its season and to bless all the work of your hand; and you shall lend to many nations, but you shall not borrow.**
>
> **Deuteronomy 28:12**

The dangers of debt are manifold. The harsh truth is that debt is the legal process by which the rich get richer and the poor get poorer. Many times it is the unfortunate result of trying to acquire wealth before it's time. It has been called a form of legal slavery, a bondage that is secured with a person's future, hopes, and dreams. Because unpaid debt accrues interest, sometimes indefinitely, it is both self-sustaining and self-reinforcing. By design, this financial arrangement can suppress a person until bankruptcy or even up until the end of their life, whichever comes first. In addition to the misery that accompanies debt, it also brings exposure to an individual's belongings:

> **Be not one of those who give pledges,**
> **who put up security for debts.**
> **If you have nothing with which to pay,**
> **why should your bed be taken from under you?**
>
> **Proverbs 22:26–27 (ESV)**

The Hebrew word for debt, *neshi*, always carries with it the idea of biting interest. For example, in 2 Kings 4:7, Elisha told the widow woman to sell the olive oil and "pay your debt." The purpose of this miracle was twofold: to free her life from the effects of biting interest and to live on the rest. It was her debt that exposed her family to slavery, and her debt needed to be eliminated before freedom and increase could come.

Debt is the leak in the bottom of a barrel or the hole in the bottom of a bag. It is a financial quicksand that fights the debtor's every effort to become freed; a black hole that sucks in resources, energy, and happiness. Debt is anti-wealth, anti-prosperity, anti-abundance, and anti-increase. It is incompatible with the Christian life, a life that should display the hallmarks of ever-increasing advancement, possessions, and abundance. Uncontrolled debt will eventually take from you all that you possess:

> **There were also those who said, "We are mortgaging our fields, our vineyards, and our houses to get grain because of the famine." And there were those who said, "We have borrowed money for the king's tax on our fields and our vineyards. Now our flesh is as the flesh of our brothers, our children are as their children. Yet we are forcing our sons**

and our daughters to be slaves, and some of our daughters have already been enslaved, but it is not in our power to help it, for other men have our fields and our vineyards.

Nehemiah 5:3–5 (ESV)

When others own your fields as a result of borrowing, only then will you realize how powerless you are to affect or change anything financially in your life. Debt sabotages the present and the future simultaneously. In a world addicted to borrowing and drowning in debt, becoming debt-free is not a popular message.

Debt offers people the illusion of wealth. But it isn't wealth. It is a mirage. Debt is a rented lifestyle, not an owned life. Perhaps the most appropriate illustration of the debt dynamic comes straight from the Bible:

> **So Shishak king of Egypt came up against Jerusalem, and took the treasures of the house of the LORD and the treasures of the king's palace. He took everything; he even took the golden shields that Solomon had made. Then King Rehoboam made shields of bronze in their place and committed them to the care of the commanders of the guard who guarded the door of the king's house.**
>
> **2 Chronicles 12:9–10**

Just as the bronze shields were substitutes for the gold shields, debt is the substitute for wealth. Gold is a heavenly material created in the stars of the universe. Bronze is an earthly alloy made from copper and tin. An ounce of gold can be worth thousands of dollars whereas an ounce of bronze is worth only pennies. Bronze is considered a scrap metal while gold is considered the currency of kings.

High-interest credit cards and long-term loans are the brass shields of today. Debt looks like a gold shield. However, over time, it will tarnish.

Debt is fake wealth.

Debt is placebo wealth.

Debt leads to poverty.

Wealth is what leads to prosperity.

Poverty versus Prosperity

Wealth, prosperity, abundance, and increase are instrumental to the life of a strong and effective Christian. As clearly and unmistakably demonstrated by Scripture, it is biblical to increase in wealth.

In order for us to make the last great advance on the earth that will culminate with the return of Jesus Christ, the church must begin to accept and wisely cultivate wealth. No longer can the church, paralyzed by fear, afford to neglect and reject the reality, promise, and power of biblical wealth, because fear is the foundation of the poverty belief system.

It is a beautiful and powerful thing when a Christian begins to harvest the economic blessings of God in his or her life. They will no longer be scared of wealth. They will cease to be intimidated by prosperity. As New Testament believers begin to understand the vital necessity of God's supernatural blessings, they will begin to understand the importance of biblically-sanctioned wealth.

It is critical that God's people increase in faith and understand the importance of prosperity, abundance, and increase and the role these blessings bring to their lives. The absence of faith for wealth is the presence of faith for poverty.

Taking Action

While it would be nice to simply sit back and rejoice about the wonderful characteristics of biblical wealth, it would not be advisable. The Bible teaches that Satan is stalking your life, seeking to devour any part of it that he can. Quite possibly the most frequent area the enemy attacks with stunning success is the finances of God's people. The Bible tells us that wealth provides security and protection. This is precisely why Satan attacks wealth with such ferocity. He wants God's people exposed, laid bare, and unprotected.

Furthermore, the Apostle Paul showed us that the purpose of wealth isn't just for the increasing of our own personal harvest, but it is also that we might be enriched for liberality toward others. The purpose of wealth is not solely for luxury and self-gratification; it was that it might be distributed to others in such a way as to cause thanksgiving to God.

Are you a giver? What is your attitude toward the poor and less fortunate? Do you view those who are struggling as less worthy of a better life? These are all questions that can only be answered by the person in the mirror.

Additionally, debt is the antithesis to wealth. They are contrasting values and the direct opposite of one another. Debt cannot be simply wished away. It must be attacked. But this is more than just the adjustment of an attitude or belief system. Real debt reduction comes as a result of lifestyle changes. It means cutting up credit cards. It means taking fewer vacations. It means splurging less on the things you don't need. It means establishing a budget and sticking to a spending plan.

Rest assured, any short-term pain will easily be eclipsed by the long-term gain.

7

THE MASTER KEY FOR ACCESSING WEALTH

When I was fourteen years old, I received a telescope for Christmas. Afterward, there were many summer nights where I could be found under the stars, studying the heavens and searching for distant galaxies. While I certainly didn't discover anything new or extraordinary, I happened upon an amazing visual phenomenon that would decades later profoundly affect my understanding of wealth acquisition.

My telescope was rather rudimentary and didn't benefit from the computerized scopes and sophisticated celestial databases found on today's modern ones. As a result, it was necessary for me to first locate with the naked eye the particular sector of the sky I was interested in viewing. In order to gather a general sense of the night sky and get a bearing on the constellation I was searching for, the telescope instructions directed me to locate a certain star before attempting to adjust the focus and other settings. It was at that time I discovered the phenomena of "averted vision."

Averted vision is a technique that uses peripheral vision for viewing faint objects. It involves not looking directly at the object being viewed, but looking a little off to the side, while continuing to concentrate on the object. I discovered, quite frustratingly, as I would attempt to focus on a distant star in the nighttime sky, that the star would suddenly and mysteriously disappear from my vision. However, when I shifted my view slightly to the left or right, the star would reappear within my peripheral vision.

The reason stars disappear when you look directly at them is because of the anatomy of the photoreceptors in your retina. We all have two types of light-sensing cells in our eyes: the rods and the cones. The cones see fine detail and color while the rods see better in dim light. Since the rods are more numerous than cones in the periphery of the retina, the easiest way to see a dim star at night is by looking at it with your peripheral vision.

Peripheral vision is a part of vision that occurs only on the side gaze. More specifically, peripheral vision is what is "seen by the side of the eye" when one is looking straight ahead. This side vision grants us the ability to see objects and activity outside of our central area of focus or direct line of sight. Peripheral vision is actually the largest part of our vision and is essential for processing both motion and orientation. Furthermore, studies have shown that one of the greatest advantages of peripheral vision is it brings with it peripheral awareness, which is crucial for our safety in dangerous situations. Research in neuroscience has revealed that the vision in the center of our visual field is much more accurate and detailed than vision in the periphery. Not surprisingly, objects that are kept in the center of our visual field are what we become "fixated" on.

It took practice, time, and patience, but eventually I learned how to use averted vision, a function of my peripheral vision, to quickly locate the star I was looking for. Little did I know that later in life, my experience and understanding with peripheral vision would result in the powerful lesson I discovered regarding biblical wealth.

I had actually long forgotten these experiences as a young astronomer until my oldest daughter recently received a telescope for her birthday. Fast forward to present day, and I found myself under the same nighttime sky with my own daughter, teaching her how to use her own childhood telescope. Together we began the process of stationing and positioning the telescope as I had done so many years ago. As the time came to center the telescope on the stars she wanted to view, I began to scan the sky with my naked eye, looking for a particular star to get my bearing. Once again, just as decades earlier, I experienced the same phenomenon of the faint star I looked at disappearing from view. Instinctively, I averted my vision slightly and the star reappeared and came back into focus.

It was at that very moment I understood the master key to accessing true biblical wealth.

Lessons from the World's Wealthiest Man

Bible historians and theologians consider King Solomon to be one of the wealthiest men who ever lived. It is estimated that Solomon possessed a peak net worth that would have surpassed two trillion dollars in today's money. His personal fortune consisted of vast amounts of gold, possessions, and land. Growing continuously as a result of expansion, taxes, and trade, the riches amassed by Solomon positioned him as one of history's wealthiest and most powerful rulers.

One night after Solomon had risen to power and assumed his father's throne, he had a fascinating encounter with God in the midst of a dream:

> In Gibeon the LORD appeared to Solomon in a dream at night; and God said, "Ask what you wish Me to give you." Then Solomon said, "You have shown great lovingkindness to Your servant David my father, according as he walked before You in truth and righteousness and uprightness of heart toward You; and You have reserved for him this great lovingkindness, that You have given him a son to sit on his throne, as it is this day. Now, O LORD my God, You have made Your servant king in place of my father David, yet I am but a little child; I do not know how to go out or come in. Your servant is in the midst of Your people which You have chosen, a great people who are too many to be numbered or counted. So give Your servant an understanding heart to judge Your people to discern between good and evil. For who is able to judge this great people of Yours?"
>
> It was pleasing in the sight of the Lord that Solomon had asked this thing. God said to him, "Because you have asked this thing and have not asked for yourself long life, nor have asked riches for yourself, nor have you asked for the life of your enemies, but have asked for yourself discernment to understand justice, behold, I have done according to your words. Behold, I have given you a wise and discerning heart, so that there has been no one like you before you, nor shall one like you arise after you. I have also given you what you have not asked, both riches and honor, so that there will not be any among the kings like you all your days. If you walk in My ways, keeping My statutes and commandments, as your father David walked, then I will prolong your days."
>
> **1 Kings 3:5–14**

During this fascinating interaction with God, King Solomon makes an amazing request. He asks God to grant him wisdom, knowledge, and an understanding heart. The king asks for God's help that he might conduct himself properly and rule over God's people effectively.

Solomon did not ask for riches.

Solomon did not ask for wealth.

Solomon's request greatly impressed God.

Second Chronicles records a similar version of the conversation:

> **"Give me now wisdom and knowledge, that I may go out and come in before this people, for who can rule this great people of Yours?" God said to Solomon, "Because you had this in mind, and did not ask for riches, wealth or honor, or the life of those who hate you, nor have you even asked for long life, but you have asked for yourself wisdom and knowledge that you may rule My people over whom I have made you king, wisdom and knowledge have been granted to you. And I will give you riches and wealth and honor, such as none of the kings who were before you has possessed nor those who will come after you."**
>
> **2 Chronicles 1:10–12**

A deeper study of King Solomon, one of the richest people in history, reveals five distinct attributes that comprise the true biblical model for wealth acquisition for us:

1. Solomon honored God's meeting place:

> **Then Solomon and all the assembly with him went to the high place which was at Gibeon, for God's tent of meeting was there, which Moses the servant of the LORD had made in the wilderness. However, David had brought up the ark of God from Kiriath-jearim to the place he had prepared**

for it, for he had pitched a tent for it in Jerusalem. Now the bronze altar, which Bezalel the son of Uri, the son of Hur, had made, was there before the tabernacle of the LORD, and Solomon and the assembly sought it out. Solomon went up there before the LORD to the bronze altar which was at the tent of meeting, and offered a thousand burnt offerings on it.

2 Chronicles 1:3–6

2. Solomon loved God with all of his heart:

Now Solomon loved the LORD, walking in the statutes of his father David.

1 Kings 3:3

3. Solomon was humble and worshipful:

When Solomon had finished praying this entire prayer and supplication to the LORD, he arose from before the altar of the LORD, from kneeling on his knees with his hands spread toward heaven.

1 Kings 8:54

4. Solomon prioritized wisdom over wealth:

In that night God appeared to Solomon and said to him, "Ask what I shall give you." Solomon said to God, "You have dealt with my father David with great lovingkindness, and have made me king in his place. Now, O LORD God, Your promise to my father David is fulfilled, for You have made me king over a people as numerous as the dust of the earth. Give me now wisdom and knowledge, that I may go

out and come in before this people, for who can rule this great people of Yours?"

2 Chronicles 1:7–10

5. Solomon was an extremely generous giver:

And King Solomon and all the congregation of Israel, who were assembled to him, were with him before the ark, sacrificing so many sheep and oxen they could not be counted or numbered.

1 Kings 8:5

King Solomon offered a sacrifice of 22,000 oxen and 120,000 sheep. Thus the king and all the people dedicated the house of God. The priests stood at their posts, and the Levites also, with the instruments of music to the LORD, which King David had made for giving praise to the LORD—"for His lovingkindness is everlasting"—whenever he gave praise by their means, while the priests on the other side blew trumpets; and all Israel was standing. Then Solomon consecrated the middle of the court that was before the house of the LORD, for there he offered the burnt offerings and the fat of the peace offerings because the bronze altar which Solomon had made was not able to contain the burnt offering, the grain offering and the fat.

2 Chronicles 7:5–7

Solomon was a man who practiced honor, love, humble worship, wisdom, and generosity. These traits are the biblical keys for wealth acquisition and form the foundation for a powerful relationship with God, a relationship that will open the doors for the Lord to do great exploits in the lives of His children.

THE MASTER KEY TO WEALTH ACQUISITION

When God said to Solomon, "Ask what you wish Me to give you," the implication was that God would grant Solomon whatever he would request. However, Solomon wasn't seeking wealth. Riches and prosperity were not the chief desires of his heart. Gold, silver, and precious jewels did not dominate his thoughts nor were those things the focus of his heart.

The master key to wealth acquisition is simply this:

Do not seek to acquire wealth.

King Solomon demonstrated that wealth, prosperity, abundance, and increase are the natural rewards of *not seeking* any of them. Jesus said it this way:

> **But seek ye first the kingdom of God, and his righteousness; and all these things shall be added unto you.**
>
> Matthew 6:33 (KJV)

In addition to granting Solomon wisdom, knowledge, and an understanding heart, God also granted him riches, wealth, and honor.

> **I have also given you what you have not asked, both riches and honor, so that there will not be any among the kings like you all your days.**
>
> 1 Kings 3:13

WEALTH MUST REMAIN PERIPHERAL

Obviously, Solomon knew that God could make him rich. The Lord made David his father rich as well as the patriarchs who had lived before him. But Solomon didn't allow wealth to become the object of his focus; he did not allow it to become his fixation. Solomon kept his vision centered on the right things — wisdom and knowledge — while keeping riches and wealth in the peripheral. We know this was the secret to Solomon's wealth because God said it was in His Word. He used his spiritual averted vision to keep riches in his peripheral vision. A deeper study of God's Word reveals all of the blessed patriarchs demonstrated the ability to keep wealth in their peripheral vision. We would be wise to follow the example King Solomon and other great men of God set before us.

It would appear the right way for tapping the world's wealth system would be for us to do it the way Solomon did. Wealth cannot be the priority of our life. It cannot become the main goal. It must be peripheral. Living a life of *not* chasing wealth is the polar opposite of how so many others live. Millions of people, including Christians, pursue wealth and money continually. Without realizing it, money has become their god. They put all of their time and energy into grasping just one more dollar. Grown adults who would appear to be mature and sensible from all outward appearances are inwardly consumed by an unquenchable desire for more money and riches. They sacrifice their families on the altar of riches. They sacrifice their health and happiness on the altar of money. No amount of money is ever enough. Their love of money sends a root of evil deep into their soul, rotting their motives and corrupting their destinies.

SEE WEALTH WITHOUT SEEKING WEALTH

Proper wealth acquisition begins the day a Christian learns how to see wealth without seeking wealth.

Therefore if you have been raised up with Christ, keep seeking the things above, where Christ is, seated at the right

hand of God. Set your mind on the things above, not on the things that are on earth.

Colossians 3:1–2

What Paul is describing in the above verse is focus. The Apostle is reminding us that our focus needs to be on the things of God rather than on the things of mankind. Part of the formula that results in biblical wealth is keeping "the things above" in the center of our vision while keeping "the things that are on earth" in our peripheral vision. This requires averting our vision. It means looking off to the side of wealth, not looking directly at it. It means leading a disciplined life where our priorities and purposes are lined up with God's plan for our lives.

The loss of peripheral vision results in a condition known as tunnel vision. Tunnel vision is a sight defect in which something cannot be properly seen unless it is in the very center of the field of view. A loss of peripheral vision occurs when a person becomes consumed with one particular object, such as money. This fixation on wealth is why so many Christians fall victim to the twin destroyers called greed and covetousness.

> **But those who want to get rich fall into temptation and a snare and many foolish and harmful desires which plunge men into ruin and destruction. For the love of money is a root of all sorts of evil, and some by longing for it have wandered away from the faith and pierced themselves with many griefs.**
>
> **1 Timothy 6:9–10**

> **Do not weary yourself to gain wealth,**
> **Cease from your consideration of it.**
> **When you set your eyes on it, it is gone.**

> **For wealth certainly makes itself wings**
> **Like an eagle that flies toward the heavens.**
>
> **Proverbs 23:4–5**

> **No servant can serve two masters; for either he will hate the one and love the other, or else he will be devoted to one and despise the other. You cannot serve God and wealth.**
>
> **Luke 16:13**

Keep in mind the above "wealth warnings" do not negate the Bible's wealth promises. The Bible is full of "sin warnings," but they do not negate the promises of salvation. God's Word includes "false teacher" warnings, but those warnings do not negate the promises of God-ordained leadership. The warnings in the Bible regarding wealth actually serve to validate and make sure the blessings of godly wealth.

God's methods for wealth acquisition are resistant to greed because His methods focus on motives, not money. Greed is condemned throughout the Bible because it is at odds with the nature of God. If you want a taste of what Solomon had, then you must do the same things that Solomon did. Practicing honor, love, humble worship, wisdom, and generosity leaves little room for greed. Generosity especially will take you straight to the top whereas greed will take you straight to the bottom.

This is God's model for wealth acquisition, and He designed it this way so as to keep our motives in check. The truth is biblical wealth, prosperity, abundance, and increase will always be about motives and not money. Impure motives are precisely why so many of God's children continue to stumble financially. It's best to be the person with one hundred dollars and the right motives than the person with one million dollars and the wrong motives.

The Pattern for Prosperity

King Solomon enjoyed enormous wealth.

He did not make riches or prosperity the focus of his life.

He did not ask for those things even after the Lord gave him the opportunity to do so.

Solomon experienced his legendary abundance and increase because he honored God's house, loved the Lord with all of his heart, was humble and worshipful, prioritized wisdom above wealth, and was a generous giver. Priorities determine either poverty or prosperity.

The master key for unlocking biblical wealth is keeping it in your side gaze, a lesson Solomon learned early on in his lifetime. As a result, he was blessed with both incredible wisdom and breathtaking riches. But even while Solomon knew that prioritizing wisdom over riches was the key to unlocking great wealth, it was his acts of giving that blew the doors open and brought him into a place of explosive returns.

Taking Action

If you want to keep wealth in your peripheral vision, you will need to learn how to avert your eyes, which takes great effort. Staying away from car dealerships isn't especially fun when you have a thing for new cars. Averting your eyes means walking past the jewelry stores, the shopping malls, and the fancy restaurants. It also means reining in your online spending habits and taking control of your impulse buying. No one said it would be easy or fun, but it will pay off in the end!

Delayed gratification refers to the ability to put off something pleasurable now in order to gain something more rewarding later. Human beings are terrible at this discipline, and Christians are no better.

However, the hard path always gets easier, and maintaining a lifestyle of delayed gratification will compound the rewards as the years go by.

Solomon was a person who honored God's house and loved the Lord with all of his heart. He was humble, worshipful, and generous; a wonderful example of a man who prioritized wisdom over wealth. It would be wise to embrace and practice the traits of Solomon on your journey to wealth, prosperity, abundance, and increase. It is entirely possible to see wealth without seeking it.

Don't ever chase after wealth.

Let God bring it to you in His timing.

8

THE SEED AND STEWARDSHIP

Located on the top of a soaring rock plateau in Israel, Masada is an ancient mountaintop fortress overlooking the Dead Sea. Constructed over two millennia ago on the edge of the Judaean Desert, it was the site of a spectacular palace built by King Herod the Great. In 66 AD, following a revolt against the Roman Empire, Masada was besieged and occupied by Jewish rebels, the Sicarii. Subsequently, in 73 AD, the Romans laid siege against Masada in order to retake the fortress and crush the resistance. Upon entering the fortress the Roman commanders discovered a vast scene of death. Rather than suffer defeat and captivity at the hands of the Romans, the remaining Jewish defenders had drawn lots and killed one another, down to the last man, who was the only one left to take his life.

In 1963, during archeological excavations at Herod's palace, site archeologists discovered a small clay jar dating back 2,000 years to the time of Masada. Inside the unearthed pot they found a small stockpile of ancient seeds. Subsequently, the seeds were cataloged and stored away at Tel Aviv's Bar-Ilan University for over forty years. However, in 2005, a botanical researcher decided to plant one of the seeds to observe what would happen after the centuries had passed.

The experiment paid off. Not only did the ancient seed sprout, it produced a sapling that had not been seen by human eyes for centuries. The Judean date palm tree, which was driven to extinction around 500 AD, lived again. The plant was nicknamed Methuselah, after the longest-lived person in the Bible. Not only has the archeological wonder continued to grow and thrive, in 2011 it produced its first flower that signaled its ability to reproduce. The date seed, preserved from the time of Jesus Christ, lay undisturbed until the Masada excavations, waiting for discovery and the right conditions for rebirth.

THE POWER OF A SEED

A seed is an embryonic plant enclosed in a protective outer covering. Seeds, which are very diverse in size, are formed in the process of plant reproduction in several groups of plants. A typical seed consists of a seed coat, the embryo, and a store of nutrients for the seedling that will grow from the embryo. The seed coat can be of various thicknesses and protects the embryo from injury, predators, and harsh environmental conditions. The protection of the embryo, coupled with the large food reserves in the seed, affords the seedling a powerful start on life. This is a mastery of design when it comes to seeds, plants, and their reproduction. Plants are like people in that they produce babies and make new plants. Simply put, a seed is a baby plant.

A seed is alive and always waiting for the right conditions to germinate and grow. In order for a seed to germinate, it requires the right kind of soil coupled with the exterior catalysts of sunlight, water, oxygen, and temperature. When the conditions are right and the seed is in the proper ground, the embryo splits the seed coat and begins to grow into the soil. As the embryo gathers water, the shoot begins to grow upward toward the light. As the stem grows, leaves develop, and roots begin to spread into the soil. As a maturing plant, the seedling makes its own food, produces fruit, and reproduces its own seeds after itself.

The Seed and Stewardship

In the Old Testament, the book of Genesis contains an explanation of how all plant life forms began:

> **Then God said, "Let the earth sprout vegetation, plants yielding seed, and fruit trees on the earth bearing fruit after their kind with seed in them"; and it was so. The earth brought forth vegetation, plants yielding seed after their kind, and trees bearing fruit with seed in them, after their kind; and God saw that it was good.**
>
> **Genesis 1:11–12**

Notice that vegetation, plants, and trees create seeds within them. This is truly an amazing thing. A small seed might seem insignificant, but the power of a seed is not in its *size*; the power of a seed is in its *potential*. Potential is what makes a seed so valuable. An apple seed carries within it the potential for thousands of apple trees. It has been rightly said that anyone can count the seeds in an apple, but no one can count the apples in a seed. Likewise, a tiny mustard seed has the potential to multiply itself 10,000 percent or more. It's important for Christians to remember that their seeds represent their potential, therefore their potential can be exponential.

Multiplying Your Supply

The biblical blueprint for seedtime and harvest is the same blueprint God has supplied regarding giving and receiving. The earth's global wealth system is governed by giving and receiving, which is also called sowing and reaping. Non-Christians only know this as buying and selling and cannot fully comprehend the depth and significance of the activity.

Paul dedicated a lengthy portion of Scripture to the topic of sowing and reaping when he wrote to explain the details of the activity to the church located in Corinth. It is in these enlightening verses that Paul describes giving as sowing and the subsequent increase as harvesting:

> **Now this I say, he who sows sparingly will also reap sparingly, and he who sows bountifully will also reap bountifully. Each one must do just as he has purposed in his heart, not grudgingly or under compulsion, for God loves a cheerful giver. And God is able to make all grace abound to you, so that always having all sufficiency in everything, you may have an abundance for every good deed; as it is written,**
>
> **"HE SCATTERED ABROAD, HE GAVE TO THE POOR, HIS RIGHTEOUSNESS ENDURES FOREVER."**
>
> **Now He who supplies seed to the sower and bread for food will supply and multiply your seed for sowing and increase the harvest of your righteousness; you will be enriched in everything for all liberality, which through us is producing thanksgiving to God.**
>
>

2 Corinthians 9:6–11

Christians do themselves a great disservice when they do not take the time to get educated about giving. It takes effort to learn about the dynamics of giving. An informed giver will know what giving is, how it works, and exactly what to expect when they give. As a result, many Christians have defaulted to a lifestyle of not giving. A prime reason that people do not engage in giving is they do not know or understand the formulas, functions, and rewards of biblical giving. For thousands of years, God has had in place a system for the financial blessing of His children, a system that is activated by giving. It is imperative people understand how this system operates since that very system is a key component of their financial increase and economic success while upon the earth.

The Seed and Stewardship

When a Christian has a biblical understanding of the logistics of giving, it will always result in a willful and eager heart to give. No longer will he or she view giving as a required burden or a pointless activity because they are fully informed of the blessings and benefits. An enlightened believer understands it is giving that massively affects their ability to make an economic difference in both the church and marketplaces of the world.

In addition to knowing what giving is, Christians must also know why they should give. According to Luke 6:38, their future wealth is directly and proportionally connected to their present giving:

> **Give, and it will be given to you. They will pour into your lap a good measure—pressed down, shaken together, and running over. For by your standard of measure it will be measured to you in return.**
>
> **Luke 6:38**

Luke 6:38 serves as a biblical model for giving. Giving is a natural action that activates a spiritual law. That, in turn, produces a natural increase. This verse is a guaranteed formula for abundance and increase. It is a blueprint for both the acquisition and multiplication of wealth. God designed giving to tap into the earth's global wealth system. The mighty and marvelous promise of this verse is clear: that the giver will experience a generous return. Not giving is financial suicide and a recipe for poverty and lack.

GIVING AND RECEIVING

Give is an interesting word. It means to freely present or deliver something that is one's own to the permanent possession of another. In general, it may also mean yielding possession of something by way of exchange. For the Christian, however, giving is the no-strings-attached release of something they have to someone else.

A closer study of the original Greek language of Luke 6:38 yields some additional insights. *Strong's Concordance* states that both times the word for *give* is used, it is the Greek word, *didómi* which also translates as "offer, put or place." However, the first "give" is a present-tense verb whereas the second "give" is a future-tense verb.

> **Give** [offer or transfer in the present]**, and it will be given** [offered or transferred in the future] **to you.**
>
> **Luke 6:38**

This is why the Scripture says, "Give, and it will be given to you." This is important to understand. The present "give" from a Christian both precedes and guarantees the future "give" from God. It would be accurate to say a future return from God is conditional upon an earlier moment of giving. A decrease always precedes an increase just as an investment always precedes a return. This is an essential component of the law of giving and is referred to in the Bible as seedtime and harvest. One of the components of seedtime and harvest is that you can only harvest what you have first planted.

OWNERSHIP VERSUS STEWARDSHIP

While examining the crucial topic of giving, it is important to understand the difference between ownership and stewardship, and especially how these truths apply to a child of God.

A fundamental problem with the concept of giving is it innocently, but mistakenly, implies ownership. This is one of the primary reasons people struggle so much with giving. Inwardly, people believe they own the things they are in possession of. While this is the prevalent mentality throughout the world, it simply is not true. People like to believe they own houses, cars, money, and other such things, but the truth is, no one actually owns anything.

In reality, people are only able to possess things, and even that is true only for a limited amount of time. The duration of time may be short or long, but it will eventually come to an end. When our time on earth is done, our possessions will move into someone else's possession. The fact is, people are just stewarding the things in their possession. This is true for every man or woman who is currently living or who has ever lived on the planet.

Ownership and stewardship are very different mindsets. Ownership is when something belongs to someone, free and clear, which gives that someone the right to do with his property whatever he desires. Stewardship, on the other hand, is managing the care of something that belongs to someone else. Notice the vast difference between those two definitions.

Ownership says, "Things belong to me." Stewardship says, "Things are entrusted to me." Ownership says, "I can do with it what I want because it belongs to me," whereas stewardship says, "I cannot do with it what I want because it belongs to someone else." Ownership says, "If I misuse this possession, it only affects me," whereas stewardship says, "If I misuse this, it affects both myself and the owner of this possession."

Although possession might imply ownership, it does not actually mean ownership. To possess something simply means you currently hold or have control over something for the duration of time that you possess it. If you were to lend your car to a friend, it does not mean they own the car just because it is now in their possession. They would quite simply, and legally, only be a steward of your car for a time. How they treat your car and the condition they return the car to you would obviously greatly affect your relationship. It would also affect your future relationship.

Christians are owners of nothing, yet we are stewards of everything. Truthfully, no Christian has, at any time, ever truly owned anything while on the planet. Every Christian who has ever lived has simply been a steward, custodian, or caretaker of possessions during their time upon the earth.

Everything Belongs to God

I'm sure you agree that everything belongs to God, which is an important precursor to understanding the topic of giving. You cannot give to God what He already owns. There are numerous verses in the Bible that designate God as the owner of everything. Consider the following passages of Scripture:

> **Behold, to the LORD your God belong heaven and the highest heavens, the earth and all that is in it.**
>
> **Deuteronomy 10:14**

> **The earth is the LORD'S, and all it contains,**
> **The world, and those who dwell in it.**
>
> **Psalm 24:1**

> **For every beast of the forest is Mine,**
> **The cattle on a thousand hills.**
> **I know every bird of the mountains,**
> **And everything that moves in the field is Mine.**
> **If I were hungry I would not tell you,**
> **For the world is Mine, and all it contains.**
>
> **Psalm 50:10–12**

> **The heavens are Yours, the earth also is Yours;**
> **The world and all it contains,**

> **You have founded them.**
>
> Psalm 89:11

> **O LORD, how many are Your works!**
> **In wisdom You have made them all;**
> **The earth is full of Your possessions.**
>
> Psalm 104:24

Lessons in Stewardship

In Matthew 25 and Luke 19, Jesus taught about the master and the nobleman who gave their servants various amounts of talents and pounds, respectively. The talents and pounds were both measurements of wealth and were entrusted to able men. However, they never really "owned" them. The talents and pounds still belonged to their respective owners. These men were simply stewards of the talents and pounds, and the master and nobleman expected them to be returned at some future point in time. It was further expected that the men would reproduce that which had been entrusted to them.

In this situation, it is important to note that the mishandling of wealth proved to be much more than about money. The mishandling of wealth actually exposed the spirit of fear in one of the servants rather than a spirit of faith. What greatly angered the master was not so much the lack of return as it was his servant not valuing what had been entrusted to him. Had the servant valued it, he would have done something with it.

We are stewards of wealth, not owners of wealth. However, God is immensely interested in how we steward that wealth. It is clear from the Bible that God has absolutely no problem channeling wealth into the hands of those who would steward it properly. It would appear that

God takes pleasure in seeing His children enjoy wealth, prosperity, and material possessions.

God determines the distribution of wealth, but we determine the increase of wealth. Those who have taken the position that we are not to increase in wealth clearly have not studied the Scriptures regarding these truths. When God said, "The gold is Mine," He was saying, "The wealth system is Mine," and it is from this wealth system that the Lord portions out His financial assignments.

Consequently, since we don't really own anything, we can't really give anything. A person cannot give something they do not own. This is not just an issue of semantics. This is addressing the foundation of having a proper mindset regarding giving. It is much easier to release something through giving when the truth of stewardship replaces the illusion of ownership.

In light of these truths, "offering" is the better word used to describe the giving process. It makes much more sense to offer up that which you have stewardship of. This is why the words "offering" and "sowing" are so incredibly important, and it is vital we understand what these words imply. Hosea 4:6 states God's people are "destroyed for lack of knowledge," and the topic of giving is a prime example where Christians lack knowledge and understanding.

God owns the cattle on a thousand hills, and He will eventually entrust some of them to you to steward. It is your stewardship of God's possessions that invites greater increase into your life. Faithful stewardship is what directs spiritual and material blessings to a child of God.

There are those who would suggest since everything belongs to God, why should we engage in what would appear to be a futile and nonessential activity? The answer is because God has called us to a life of faith and obedience to His commandments. Also, giving is one of the primary ways He is able to judge the levels of our faith and love for Him and our fellow man. Finally, giving is an action that brings us into alignment with God's own nature while serving as the mechanism for extracting increase from the earth's global wealth system.

Taking Action

A seed is quite possibly one of the most amazing things on the planet. A recent experiment demonstrated how one grain of wheat produced a stalk with an average of 55 kernels. When every kernel was planted and subsequently harvested for four consecutive seasons, the gain was over nine million kernels of wheat, a yield of over 600 pounds. This is the potential of a single seed of wheat in just four years.

Ask yourself this question: "What am I sowing?"

Everything that you do is a seed. This is so much more than what you do with your money. It is reflected in how you speak to others. Your seed is seen in how you treat your spouse and the time you invest in your children. The truth is, we are sowing seed everywhere and at all times.

We sow seed into our workplace.

We sow seed into the marketplace.

We sow seed into our social circles.

We sow seed into our families.

We sow seed into the church.

As a steward, you are not an owner of seed. The Bible teaches us that our finances are a seed, which makes all of us seed managers. Where you plant your finances is a big deal. Every penny you spend is an investment in something.

What does it say about Christians when they choose to invest more in sports and entertainment than they do in their churches? What kind of agenda is exposed when God's children set aside more time budgeting for their vacations than they do budgeting for eternity?

When you consider the enormous reproductive potential of one seed of wheat, your heart begins to comprehend the scope of Jesus' words recorded in Mark 4:8: "Other seeds fell into the good soil, and as they grew up and increased, they yielded a crop and produced thirty, sixty, and a hundredfold."

But it will never happen in your life if you don't start sowing seed.

9

WEALTH DESTRUCTION AND THE BATTLE FOR YOUR PROSPERITY

Approximately six hundred miles due west of Ecuador's coast is an isolated chain of islands that rise majestically from the vastness of the Pacific Ocean. Straddling the earth's equator, and not far from South America, the Galápagos Islands are unlike any place on earth. It is a world of ever-changing extremes formed in and around the peaks and calderas of huge active underground volcanoes. In addition to thirteen main islands, more than one hundred tiny isles, reefs, and rocks make up the Galápagos. A dazzling diversity of vibrant landscapes are splashed across this subtropical paradise accompanied by myriads of plant and animal species not found anywhere else on the planet.

One of the islands' top predators is the Galápagos hawk. Being the only resident hawk with no natural enemies, this stealthy hunter has the run of the islands. One of the hawk's primary prey is the female marine iguana. During the cold and dry season, these iguanas are forced to leave the safety of the coast, with its rocks of refuge and population of companions, so they might lay their eggs at the island's interior in the soft volcanic soil. Consequently, their journeys involve venturing hundreds of yards inland. Female iguanas lay several eggs and usually guard their burrows for days. Throughout this entire cycle, the hawk is perched high above, patiently watching and waiting for an opportunity to strike.

Eventually, weakened from hunger and fatigue, the iguanas have no choice but to return to the coast. This, however, means exposure to both the elements and their adversary. As the iguanas begin their trek back to the shore, the hawk singles out a female lingering behind the community of other iguanas, now far from the safety of her burrow. The bird begins its deadly dive. As the iguana catches sight of the descending hawk, she begins to scamper, clumsily, as fast as she can over the hot volcanic rocks and pebbles. The mighty bird swoops in, talons extended, and drops suddenly and violently upon the back of the terrified iguana.

With its wings now retracted and its full weight bearing down, the hawk forces the iguana deep into the hot sand, which quickly raises her body temperature. The fighting and resistance are fierce at first, a battle that slowly morphs into a helpless struggle, and one that ultimately results in still silence. In the end, the iguana perishes from exhaustion, the inescapable result of overwhelming heat and pressure. The iguana has become an innocent participant in the circle of life. It has also become the hawk's next meal. Ultimately, the iguana's nest lays defenseless, exposed for the inevitable invasion where her eggs will be stolen and destroyed.

An Economic Assault

I was greatly impacted when first viewing this event on a National Geographic documentary featuring the Galápagos Islands. As a lifelong pastor, I couldn't help but see the obvious similarities between these natural conflicts in the wild and the supernatural conflicts faced by Christians in their daily lives. Almost immediately, I began to see how this battle in the wild paralleled the battle for wealth waged against God's people.

This daily battle that takes place between these two natural enemies, the Galápagos hawk and the marine iguana, is a perfect illustration of the battles that transpire between a child of God and the enemies of divine inheritance. The iguana represents the modern-day Christian, pregnant with the biblical promises of wealth, prosperity, abundance, and increase. The journey, like that of the iguana's, plunges them into the harshest of environments where opponents and challenges abound. Their path forces them from the predictable safety of their comfort zones into an unpredictable arena of guaranteed warfare. The reward, if they persevere, is the enjoyment of prosperity and ever-increasing abundance.

In like manner, the hawk would represent the relentless opposition of Satan and the unpredictable circumstances of life. It is also indicative of the strife and friction generated by the jealousy and envy of financial philistines that wish failure upon us. In a subtler sense, the hawk also represents the unfortunate consequences of bad economic decisions and the innocent choices one makes while inexperienced or ignorant of the truth. The goal of these various hostilities and the goal of the hawk is one and the same: to deliver total economic defeat through exhaustion and overwhelming pressure. And just like the hawk, these outside forces descend suddenly upon God's children with incredible ferocity, attempting to steal and destroy the promises and hope of their God-given inheritances.

Christians regularly forfeit their inheritances as a result of the exhaustion and pressure experienced while battling Satan over these promises of abundance. This should not come as a surprise.

Approximately 2,500 years ago, Daniel forewarned that a tactic of the enemy in the last days would be to wear out the saints:

And he shall speak great words against the most High, and shall wear out the saints of the most High, and think to change times and laws.

Daniel 7:25 (KJV)

If the battle for souls is the most important fight ever fought – which it is — the battle for wealth is second. Wealth, prosperity, abundance, and increase are life-changing resources and powerful promises from God. They are under constant assault. Every great promise from God has always faced massive opposition, and this has never been truer than with the important and powerful promises that form the foundation for biblical wealth. Satan will never allow you to walk in wealth without a battle, and he will exert all of his strength in his efforts to lock you out of God's proven wealth system. The enormous significance of wealth becomes evident by the massive resistance an individual experiences while cultivating it.

Historically, scriptures that address the topics of wealth and prosperity have been consistently twisted and taken out of context by the ignorant and unscrupulous. This has resulted in these essential promises that are critical to a Christian's success being frequently misunderstood, ridiculed, and rejected. People will always repel from that which they do not understand.

Also, many of God's children allow the concepts of wealth and prosperity to intimidate them, causing them to cower and suffer under a dark cloud of scarcity and insufficiency, hoping luck or chance will magically improve things. Making matters even worse, they are surrounded by unbelievers – and sometimes fellow Christians — who are relentlessly critical of their faith in God to bless them materially.

As a minister for the better part of my life, it has been my observation that far too many Christians live their lives crisis to crisis, struggling in a financial rut while barely making ends meet. They simply exist in a daze of debt, hoping and praying that some day soon their ship will come in.

Subsequently, many in the church today end up in either one of two ditches. Those in one ditch angrily and vehemently deny prosperity. In doing so, they unwittingly adopt a poverty mentality; a mindset that eventually results in a life of lack. Sadly, they identify that stance as godly.

Those in the opposite ditch unashamedly embrace prosperity, but with selfish motives. Those who do so create a life that worships and serves riches, which Jesus condemned. Coincidentally, this group will also label their stance as godly.

Neither of these ditches are God's will for His people. A balanced Christian is neither brainwashed by the lies of lack nor drunken with the promises of riches. Balance is necessary to counter Satan's ferocity and stave off his efforts to devour your inheritance.

> **Be sober [well balanced and self-disciplined], be alert and cautious at all times. That enemy of yours, the devil, prowls around like a roaring lion [fiercely hungry], seeking someone to devour.**
>
> **1 Peter 5:8 (AMP)**

Satan knows it is much easier to take advantage of an unbalanced and biblically uneducated Christian more than it is one who has been balanced and educated.

STOLEN WEALTH

Satan wants to steal your wealth and rob you of your inheritance. He is the sworn enemy of your prosperity, abundance, and increase and knows that stealing it from you is the same thing as stealing it from God. Satan, like a predator, will attempt to seize your crown of wealth and extinguish your financial blessings through exhaustion and pressure.

There are also many other tools the enemy uses to steal a Christian's wealth. His tactics include doubt, opposition, persecution, mistakes, embarrassment, intimidation, wrong thinking, and false doctrine. One of Satan's most effective strategies is his tireless effort to keep Christians ignorant of God's promises:

My people are destroyed for lack of knowledge.

Hosea 4:6 (KJV)

Regardless of the method employed by Satan, his ultimate goal is to leave you exposed, without resources, and living in lack. He will abuse you, persecute you, and attempt to deceive you to the point you willingly surrender the goodness of God. He is the enemy of abundant life, a skilled expert at tricking God's children into severing themselves from heaven's supply lines.

The thief comes only to steal and kill and destroy; I came that they may have life, and have it abundantly.

John 10:10

Satan will always target that which is dearest to God's heart and valuable to God's people. Whether it is the Garden of Eden, the Promise Land or the strength of Samson, Bible history is filled with examples that demonstrate how tirelessly the enemy strives to sever people from what God has blessed them with. From Genesis through Revelation, there is a never-ending war against prosperity. Throughout the dispensations, the giving nature of God is contrasted by the stealing nature of Satan.

In Bible times, a conquest was not considered complete until the wealth of the defeated had been transferred into the hands of the conqueror. The loss of wealth always weakens people and is accompanied by exposure and shame. This remains true in modern times as well and can been seen in the tattered and ruined economies of defeated nations following the loss of a battle.

There is a long history of theft throughout the Bible. The wealth of God's people has always been robbed and ravaged. The Old Testament contains numerous examples of Israel's gold, wealth, and assets being plundered by their enemies during times of war or great conflict. The lessons to be gleaned from these examples of the past are powerful and should serve to educate and instruct God's people in the here and now.

Now these things happened to them as an example, and they were written for our instruction, upon whom the ends of the ages have come.

1 Corinthians 10:11

A History of Theft

One of the most heart-wrenching examples of Israel's devastation was the defeat they suffered at the hands of Nebuchadnezzar, the king of the Babylonians. In a series of three devastating invasions, Nebuchadnezzar laid siege to Jerusalem and Judah, completely stripping them of their wealth and power.

Years earlier, Jeremiah had prophesied the ransacking of Judah:

> I will also give over all the wealth of this city, all its produce and all its costly things; even all the treasures of the kings of Judah I will give over to the hand of their enemies, and they will plunder them, take them away and bring them to Babylon.
>
> Jeremiah 20:5

This prophecy was later fulfilled with the total looting of God's house:

> Now the bronze pillars which belonged to the house of the LORD and the stands and the bronze sea, which were in the house of the LORD, the Chaldeans broke in pieces and carried all their bronze to Babylon. They also took away the pots, the shovels, the snuffers, the basins, the pans and all the bronze vessels which were used in temple service. The captain of the guard also took away the bowls, the firepans, the basins, the pots, the lampstands, the pans and the drink offering bowls, what was fine gold and what was fine silver.
>
> Jeremiah 52:17–19

> He carried out from there all the treasures of the house of the LORD, and the treasures of the king's house, and cut in pieces all the vessels of gold which Solomon king of Israel had made in the temple of the LORD, just as the LORD had said.
>
> 2 Kings 24:13

> All the articles of the house of God, great and small, and the treasures of the house of the LORD, and the treasures of the king and of his officers, he brought them all to Babylon.
>
> 2 Chronicles 36:18

Daniel, who was taken captive and carried away to Babylon, was an eyewitness to the plundering:

> **In the third year of the reign of Jehoiakim king of Judah, Nebuchadnezzar king of Babylon came to Jerusalem and besieged it. The Lord gave Jehoiakim king of Judah into his hand, along with some of the vessels of the house of God; and he brought them to the land of Shinar, to the house of his god, and he brought the vessels into the treasury of his god.**
>
> Daniel 1:1–2

The Lord's anger is always fiercely kindled against those who would dare to carry away the treasures of God's house. Not only were the treasures of the temple spoiled, but also the treasures of the king's palace in Judah. It was customary among the heathen to display the spoils of war as presents to their gods. These enemies had taken away the gold and treasures God had bestowed upon His people, and they put them into their idols' temples. The rich vessels of God were stolen away and hung in heathen temples as trophies, a common custom among ancient nations. They were also put into idolatrous service, a use they were not purposed for. God viewed this as an evil against Himself, the One Who claimed, "the gold is Mine."

Ultimately, Jerusalem was utterly plundered and burned to the ground. Every last piece of gold, silver, and bronze was taken. Except for the poorest of the land, nothing was left behind. The terrible siege by the Babylonians under Nebuchadnezzar and subsequent destruction of Jerusalem was one of the most horrific events in the history of God's people. The extent of Israel's loss was staggering.

The Stolen Ark of the Covenant

Other examples cited in the Bible reaffirm the enemy's insatiable desire for the wealth of God's people. Following a pivotal battle between the Israelites and the Philistines, the victorious Philistines took the golden Ark of the Covenant:

> **So the Philistines fought and Israel was defeated, and every man fled to his tent; and the slaughter was very great, for there fell of Israel thirty thousand foot soldiers. And the ark of God was taken; and the two sons of Eli, Hophni and Phinehas, died.**
>
> **1 Samuel 4:10–11**

The Stolen Treasures of Jerusalem

In 2 Chronicles 12, King Shishak of Egypt waged war against Jerusalem, a battle that ultimately resulted in the plundering of their wealth:

> **So Shishak king of Egypt came up against Jerusalem, and took the treasures of the house of the LORD and the treasures of the king's palace.**
>
> **2 Chronicles 12:9**

The Stolen Fortunes of Judah

While rebuking and assigning judgment to those who had stolen the wealth of Judah and Jerusalem, the Bible records:

> **Since you have taken My silver and My gold, brought My precious treasures to your temples, and sold the sons of Judah and Jerusalem to the Greeks in order to remove them far from their territory, behold, I am going to arouse them**

from the place where you have sold them, and return your recompense on your head.

Joel 3:5–7

THE PERSECUTION OF THE EARLY CHURCH

These assaults against the children of God have continued down through the centuries. In the church's infancy, many times those who opposed the church were authorized to seize the wealth, land, and assets of Christians. Paul, prior to his conversion, was involved in the severe persecution of the church as well, even obtaining letters for the purpose of disrupting the lives of Christians by dragging them off to prison.

During the first centuries of the early church, the persecution of Christians in the Roman Empire was carried out by the state, and also by local authorities, as they deemed necessary. An empire-wide persecution of the church began in the third century leading to not only the confiscation of Christians' wealth, but of their lives as well. Numerous emperors took great advantage of the horrible persecution of Christians by stripping them of their wealth, land, and earthly possessions.

THE STOLEN WEALTH OF THE HOLOCAUST

From 1941 to 1945, during the unspeakable atrocities of the Holocaust, Nazi Germany and its collaborators systematically murdered some six million Jews. During this horrific chapter in world history, Nazi Germany instituted the practice of looting their victims' gold jewelry and wealth. The gold rings taken from concentration camp victims were used to finance the Nazi economy and even involved the barbaric practice of extracting gold fillings from the teeth of Jewish people. The total value of all assets stolen from God's people by Nazi Germany remains uncertain, but conservative studies place the numbers well into the hundreds of millions of dollars.

THE FUTURE PLUNDERING OF ISRAEL'S WEALTH

Not surprisingly, efforts to steal the wealth of God's people will continue into the future. Referring to events that have yet to unfold in the last days, Ezekiel prophesied regarding the enemies that will come together to invade the land of Judea. In what will be one of the last great conflicts of the world, distant nations conspire to seize Israel's wealth:

> **Thus says the Lord GOD, "It will come about on that day, that thoughts will come into your mind and you will devise an evil plan, and you will say, 'I will go up against the land of unwalled villages. I will go against those who are at rest, that live securely, all of them living without walls and having no bars or gates, to capture spoil and to seize plunder, to turn your hand against the waste places which are now inhabited, and against the people who are gathered from the nations, who have acquired cattle and goods, who live at the center of the world.' Sheba and Dedan and the merchants of Tarshish with all its villages will say to you, 'Have you come to capture spoil? Have you assembled your company to seize plunder, to carry away silver and gold, to take away cattle and goods, to capture great spoil?'"**
>
> **Ezekiel 38:10–13**

The Bible unequivocally states there will be those in the days we are living in who will devise plans to come against God's people who live safe and secure, all with the purpose of capturing their spoil and seizing their prosperity.

PLUNDERING YOUR OWN PROSPERITY

One of the most tragic methods by which wealth is stolen today is when Christians willingly forfeit it themselves without even so much as a struggle. Many in the church continue to plunder themselves in this destructive manner.

Not only have modern-day denominations staunchly aligned themselves against prosperity, they have gone as far as to introduce and promote vows of poverty to God's people, presenting them as holy and just.

Church history revisionists have persuaded millions of Christians that they come from a history of blessed financial poverty, while in fact, according to the Bible, the very opposite is true. Educated "theologians" teach we come from a lineage of poverty when, in reality, the true theology of God's Word records a history of wealth. Embracing a poverty mindset is an irrational and unbiblical coping mechanism, one that spirals downward into the vicious cycle of economic defeat, a quagmire that can last a lifetime.

Fear also sabotages wealth acquisition. In Matthew 25, the wicked and lazy servant took his master's gold talent and, out of fear, went and buried it in the ground. Jesus subsequently condemned this action because God is not interested in His people burying their wealth, but rather increasing it. Those who are motivated by fear and bury their wealth will never see a return because, in reality, the burying of wealth is the removal of it from God's global wealth system. Those who do not appreciate their present relationship with wealth will always sabotage their future relationship with it as well.

The willful surrender of prosperity and the complete acceptance of lack is the polar opposite of the Bible's stance on wealth and should be called out for what it really is: self-sabotage. It is a spiritual type of

Stockholm Syndrome in which Christians, as financial hostages, have developed a psychological alliance with Satan, who they have allowed to become their economic captor.

Church history vividly demonstrates there is a battle for your wealth. Satan wants your wealth and he will try and take it by deception, by theft, or by force. Modern-day events demonstrate that nothing has changed. Satan has stolen it from your forefathers. He has stolen it from those around you. And if you allow him, he will steal it from your future and children's futures as well.

Satan will never rest until he has intercepted every possible blessing the Lord has directed your way from His global wealth system.

Taking Action

Are you angry at Satan?

I sure hope so.

His methodical, ruthless, and unending assault against the goodness of God is stunning. If you are waiting for the enemy to give you a break and let you catch your breath, you are going to be waiting a very long time.

It will never happen.

Of all the ways listed above that your prosperity can be plundered, the most dangerous one is when you do it to yourself. Jesus called the man who buried his talent a wicked and lazy servant. Laziness is the unwillingness to exert energy or do work. The following is a brutal question, but one you must eventually ask yourself:

"Am I lazy?"

The honest answer to that three-word question will change the course and direction of your life. The book of Proverbs has a lot to say about laziness, but perhaps the most applicable verse for our purposes is this:

> **Being lazy will make you poor, but diligent hands bring riches.**
>
> **Proverbs 10:4 (GNT)**

10

How God Defends Your Crown

It is profoundly disturbing that any serious student of the Bible could arrive at the conclusion that God is not concerned about the wealth and prosperity of His people. The Lord's heart concerning the assets of His children, with which He Himself has blessed them with, is clearly outlined in the Bible from Genesis to Revelation.

There are seven primary redemptive names for God, and each of these names reveal a distinctive facet of His character. One of the redemptive names of God is *Jehovah Jirah*, which means *the Lord will provide*. God shows His love and compassion for us through His provision.

> Do not worry then, saying, "What will we eat?" or "What will we drink?" or "What will we wear for clothing?" For the Gentiles eagerly seek all these things; for your heavenly Father knows that you need all these things. But

seek first His kingdom and His righteousness, and all these things will be added to you.

Matthew 6:31–33

And God is able to make all grace abound to you, so that always having all sufficiency in everything, you may have an abundance for every good deed.

2 Corinthians 9:8

And my God will supply all your needs according to His riches in glory in Christ Jesus.

Philippians 4:19

In addition to being our provider, God also offers us protection from the enemies we will face in this life. Another redemptive name for God is *Jehovah Nissi*, which means *the Lord is my Banner*. This name declares God's protection, leadership, and deliverance for His people. As our protector, God is able to shield us against Satan's efforts of trying to steal our provisions along with any other forces and obstacles that would rise up against our blessings.

The principle of supernatural asset protection is set forth in the life-impacting verses located in the book of Malachi:

> "Bring the whole tithe into the storehouse, so that there may be food in My house, and test Me now in this," says the LORD of hosts, "if I will not open for you the windows of heaven and pour out for you a blessing until it overflows. Then I will rebuke the devourer for you, so that it will not destroy the fruits of the ground; nor will your vine in the field cast its grapes," says the LORD of hosts. "All the

nations will call you blessed, for you shall be a delightful land," says the LORD of hosts.

Malachi 3:10–12

Referencing the Lord's promise to rebuke Satan, *Matthew Poole's Commentary* says God will "lay a restraint upon" and "prohibit" all kinds of devourers, no matter how mighty or incredible in multitude they may be. "A rebuke from God will check them all at once as if they were but one." It is evident the Lord is concerned with His people's wealth and goods not becoming consumed by their enemies. Jehovah Nissi is the protector of your crown. What God provides, God will also protect.

Furthermore, God's nature is unchanging:

For I, the LORD, do not change.

Malachi 3:6

Jesus Christ is the same yesterday and today and forever.

Hebrews 13:8

Every good gift and every perfect gift is from above, coming down from the Father of lights, with whom there is no variation or shadow due to change.

James 1:17 (ESV)

GOD'S PROTECTION PLAN

God has not changed, so we can rest assured His heart has remained unchanged as well. What God did for His people long ago He will still do for His people today. God has graciously blessed us with so much, and if we really want to know how the Lord feels about the things He has given to us, we need to look no further than the Bible. There is much scriptural precedence in God's Word regarding the topic of wealth protection. The scriptures are full of powerful and illustrative examples of God's benevolent financial protection and restoration.

Fortunately, by taking an unfiltered and unashamed look at the examples found in the Bible, we are able to see the steps God takes in order to keep the crown of wealth securely upon the heads of His children. How does God deal with loss and lack? How does He feel about the theft and destruction of His peoples' wealth? What efforts does God undertake in order to bring miraculous restoration and provision back into the lives of His people?

Regarding Stolen Property

God takes a hard stand against theft. The commandment, "Thou shalt not steal" forbids the unjust taking or keeping the goods of another or wronging them in any way in respect to their goods. God demands that people respect and honor the possessions of others, and this commandment therefore prohibits all forms of theft. God's stance on the property rights of others is severe, even including the complete destitution of a thief in order to make things right:

> **But if he is caught, he must pay back seven times what he stole, even if he has to sell everything in his house.**
>
> **Proverbs 6:31 (NLT)**

During a difficult time in the life of David, he and his men came to the city of Ziklag only to discover it had been raided and burned to the ground by the Amalekites. Although none of their families had been killed, all had been taken captive, young and old alike. It was at this moment that David and his men lifted up their voices and wept until they had no more strength left to weep. The loss and despair was so great, some of the people even began to speak of stoning David. His ability to survive the crisis came only through him encouraging himself and finding strength in the Lord God.

In 1 Samuel, it states that David then came before God and asked if he should pursue the adversaries that had plundered them:

> **David inquired of the LORD, saying, "Shall I pursue this band? Shall I overtake them?" And He said to him, "Pursue, for you will surely overtake them, and you will surely rescue all."**
>
> 1 Samuel 30:8

The Lord told David to pursue his enemies, and in doing so, he would recover everything that had been taken from them. David and four hundred men began pursuit and eventually overtook the Amalekites. They found them eating, drinking, and dancing because of the great spoil they had taken from the land of Judah. An extended battle ensued, and David slaughtered all those who had plundered he and his people. As a result of David's victory, he was able to recover all that the Amalekites had taken. In the end, absolutely nothing of theirs was missing of the spoils that had been stolen. David took it all back. Additionally, David captured all the sheep and cattle that belonged to the Amalekites, which the people referred to as "David's spoil."

The Lord defended David's wealth and caused it to be returned to him.

Regarding Bad Investments

Second Chronicles records the historical account of King Amaziah's efforts to assemble 300,000 of his soldiers from Judah for an impending battle. As part of Amaziah's plans, he hired an additional 100,000 valiant warriors out of Israel for 100 talents of silver. But a man of God came to Amaziah and warned him not to take the army of Israel with him because the Lord had refused to help anyone from Israel at that time. The man warned Amaziah that even if he fought hard, if he did it alongside the 100,000 warriors he had hired, he would be defeated by his enemies. Almost immediately, Amaziah regretted his financial investment:

> **Amaziah said to the man of God, "But what shall we do for the hundred talents which I have given to the troops of Israel?" And the man of God answered, "The LORD has much more to give you than this."**
>
>

2 Chronicles 25:9

As King Amaziah learned, financial regret is the fruit of bad financial decisions. But the Bible says, "The Lord has much more to give you than this." Bad investments are nothing to God, and He has much more to give you than you could possibly ever lose.

Regarding Debt Cancellation

On a sad day, the wife of one of the sons of the prophets brought her plea to Elisha. She informed him that her husband, who was also Elisha's servant, had died. This widow's husband was a godly man and a servant who feared the Lord. But his unexpected death left her carrying overwhelming debt. Making matters even worse, the creditor she owed was threatening to take her two children away as his slaves.

Elisha asked the widow what things she still had in her house. Her response was that she "had nothing in the house except a jar of oil." Elisha then instructed her to go out and borrow as many empty containers as she could from all of her friends and neighbors. He told her once she had done that to enter her home, shut the door, and begin pouring from the single jar of oil into all the vessels she had gathered. As her and her sons began to pour the oil, they discovered to their joy and amazement that the oil never ran out. Through her act of faith, each and every container was filled.

> **So she went from him and shut the door behind her and her sons; they were bringing *the vessels* to her and she poured. When the vessels were full, she said to her son, "Bring me another vessel." And he said to her, "There is not one vessel more." And the oil stopped. Then she came and told the man of God. And he said, "Go, sell the oil and pay your debt, and you *and* your sons can live on the rest."**
>
> 2 Kings 4:5–7

God graciously rescued this woman from certain calamity. It should be noted that, in addition to eliminating her debt, this miracle also provided the money she and her sons would need to live on in the future. In truth, what God gifted to her was a fully funded retirement plan.

Regarding Restoration

In the Gospel of Luke, Jesus shares a story with those who had gathered to hear Him. The Lord spoke of a man who had two sons, and how one day the younger one came to his father requesting the share of the estate. The father divided his property between his sons, and, not long after, the younger son gathered together everything he owned and set off for a distant country.

After arriving in that country, he quickly squandered all of his wealth in wild and riotous living. The Bible states that "after he had spent everything," a severe famine came upon the whole country. This greatly magnified the need and lack of the man insomuch that he went and hired himself out to a citizen who, in turn, sent him to feed the pigs in his field. It became so bad that he would have been glad to eat what the pigs were eating, but no one gave him a thing.

After coming to his senses, the young man realized that even the servants in his father's house have food to spare while here he was starving to death. He determined to return to his father, repent of his foolishness, and beg to be treated as a hired servant. So he arose, left the pigs and poverty behind, and began the journey back to his father.

> **So he got up and came to his father. But while he was still a long way off, his father saw him and felt compassion for him, and ran and embraced him and kissed him. And the son said to him, "Father, I have sinned against heaven and in your sight; I am no longer worthy to be called your son." But the father said to his slaves, "Quickly bring out the best robe and put it on him, and put a ring on his hand and sandals on his feet; and bring the fattened calf, kill it, and let us eat and celebrate; for this son of mine was dead and has come to life again; he was lost and has been found." And they began to celebrate.**
>
> Luke 15:20–24

The account of the prodigal son vividly describes a unique result of God's goodness — the undeserved and fortunate outcome of the son's stupidity, arrogance, and pride. It is also a story that displays the heart of God through the process of an amazing restoration.

Regarding Job Protection

As Elisha's ministry was growing, the time came when the sons of the prophets began discussing the need for a larger place to meet. After being told that the place had become too small for all of them, Elisha dispatched his servants to the Jordan for the purpose of harvesting trees and lumber for the construction of a larger meeting place. Following the decision to relocate their ministry base, Elisha made the decision to go with them.

After reaching the Jordan, the project commenced with the cutting down of the trees. While one of the young prophets was cutting, the ax head on the ax he was using suddenly detaches and is flung into the river. Surprised and dismayed at the loss of the ax head, the man yells out to Elisha for help, further adding that the ax was borrowed.

> **Then the man of God said, "Where did it fall?" When he showed him the place, he cut off a stick and threw it in there and made the iron float. And he said, "Take it up." So he reached out his hand and took it.**
>
> **2 Kings 6:6–7**

This account is scriptural precedence that God will not only protect your assets, He will protect your employment as well. God cares about even the seemingly smallest asset and will expend miraculous power to retrieve possessions that are accidentally lost.

Regarding Attacks from the Enemy

Job was a man who was blameless and upright, a person who feared God and shunned evil. He was so exceedingly blessed in his times — both financially and materially — that he was considered the greatest of all the people of the east. Job loved God and continually offered burnt offerings to the Lord on the behalf of his family.

When Satan brought his assault against Job, it was one that was unequaled in its ferocity in the history of mankind. Satan's assailing of Job was legendary, resulting not only in the murder of Job's sons and daughters, but also in the death of his servants and theft of his flocks. Throughout it all, Job maintained his integrity and did not sin or charge God with wrong. Subsequently, Satan struck Job with loathsome, painful sores from the soles of his feet to the top of his head. Making matters worse, Job's wife encouraged him to "curse God and die." Yet, through it all, Job did not sin against God with his lips. The suffering and torment that Job endured most likely eclipsed even that which the strongest person could withstand.

Job held fast to his unshakable faith in God, and, as a result, not only did the Lord heal his body but also restored all the fortunes of Job. Beyond that, the Lord also increased all that Job previously had by twofold. Job was consoled and comforted following the adversities that had come upon him, and family and friends blessed him with money and gold.

> **The LORD blessed the latter days of Job more than his beginning; and he had 14,000 sheep and 6,000 camels and 1,000 yoke of oxen and 1,000 female donkeys. He had seven sons and three daughters.**
>
> Job 42:12–13

While Job's affliction is an extreme example of Satan's brutality, it serves as a comforting reminder of God's love and concern for His people, especially in times of hardship and loss.

God Is Your Defender

You have been crowned with wealth. The importance and power of prosperity, abundance, and increase cannot be overstated. From the moment God placed Adam and Eve in the Garden of Eden and continuing straight on through into present day, the Lord has defended the blessings of His people.

The earth's global wealth system was created with the purpose of perpetual increase and distribution of God's resources throughout the planet, and He will not allow Satan to rob you blind. Not only did the Lord bless the earth with wealth, He engineered marvelous ways for His people to tap into that system for their growth, security, and betterment!

TAKING ACTION

Asset protection is the techniques and strategic actions taken to protect a person's assets. The goal of this type of protection planning is to insulate oneself from those who might attempt to lay claim to your goods.

Having thoroughly examined the supernatural side of asset protection, it is vitally important to examine the natural side. The best offense is always a good defense. There are a whole lot of people in the world who are really good at making money, yet they are a train wreck when it comes to protecting it. It makes no sense to prosper and increase in wealth and abundance if you leave your assets unprotected, just waiting for Satan to sink his teeth into.

Benjamin Franklin said, "If you fail to plan, you plan to fail." Although people don't set out planning to fail, too many times failure is the result of poor planning, wrong priorities, and a lack of self-discipline. Proper planning is not just essential for success, but also for sustaining that same success.

What targets have you presented for Satan to shoot at?

It is not a lack of faith to put together an estate plan. Do you have a will in place? How about a living trust? Do you and your spouse have advanced directives and durable power of attorneys drawn up? Do you need guardianship designations? Is your health insurance sufficient? Have you taken the time to consider future scenarios and make the adjustments needed to navigate any foreseeable challenges? Don't put your family through the expensive and exhaustive process of probate court. The deathbed is the wrong time and place to begin financial planning. That is like waiting to build a boat until the tsunami is already headed for the shore.

Do you have an emergency fund in place? The majority of bankruptcies occur today as a result of people not having enough money on hand to weather a short-term financial storm. Are you positioned to financially survive an automobile breakdown or a health crisis? If your dishwasher breaks down, will you lose all hope for tomorrow?

What does your credit score look like? Is it good or bad? Your credit score is a window into your financial life.

Are you positioned to survive a financial crisis on a personal level? How about one on a national level? What would you do if an economic crisis were to strike on a global level?

As a pastor, it has been my observation that if Christians spent as much time structuring their finances as they did complaining about them, the story of their lives would be much different and greatly improved!

God stands ready to defend your crown.

How about you?

11

THE POWER TO MAKE WEALTH

In the early morning hours of September 1, 1859, a London astronomer named Richard Carrington was sketching a cluster of massive dark spots he observed scattered across the surface of the sun. Suddenly, through a brass telescope in his private observatory, he witnessed two brilliant white and intense eruptions of light from within the sunspots. The unexpected bursts of light were solar flares, unleashing the energy of ten billion atomic bombs. The enormous coronal mass ejection lasted for five minutes. Then, a few hours later, colorful auroras began to brighten the nighttime sky across the earth. Birds began to sing. Workers arose to begin their day. Some even thought it might be the end of the world.

The resulting geomagnetic storm, later named the "Carrington Effect," had begun pummeling the planet. As the day wore on, telegraphs around the world began to short-circuit and fail. History books record that telegraph lines across North America were rendered inoperable as the resulting solar storms wreaked havoc on the planet's communications technology, still in its infancy. Terminal operators experienced electric shocks and burns. Telegraph paper smoked and combusted. Communication lines across the nation were hastily disconnected from batteries. The immense electrical current surging through the wires was so powerful it risked melting the platinum contacts.

When American Telegraph Company employees in Boston arrived for work the next day, they made an amazing discovery. With batteries still disconnected following the prior day's events, they found they were able to effectively transmit telegraph messages to neighboring states using the current in the very atmosphere.

The entire atmosphere had become a conduit for communication as a result of the air being supercharged with power.

This is exactly how biblical wealth operates. And when it erupts, it does so suddenly, brilliantly, powerfully, and sometimes even unexpectedly. Prosperity, abundance, and increase will affect everything in their vicinity. In doing so, these blessings invade and supercharge a Christian's economic atmosphere. Biblical wealth permeates and saturates people, surroundings, and circumstances. And, as demonstrated in the Bible, the release of this power sparks acceleration, momentum, and accumulation.

The creation of biblical wealth is a supernatural phenomenon that can be experienced by any who are both willing and obedient to the Word of God. The experience simply cannot be explained. It must be lived.

Wealth Is Strength

> But you shall remember the LORD your God, for it is He who is giving you power to make wealth, that He may confirm His covenant which He swore to your fathers, as it is this day.
>
> **Deuteronomy 8:18**

In an earlier chapter, we saw how the Lord blessed His people with the power, or ability, to acquire strength through wealth. The implications of Deuteronomy 8:18 are enormous. It means living a life without poverty, destitution, or lack. It means banishing forever an existence of scarcity, shortage, and insufficiency. It means replacing vows of poverty with vows of prosperity. It means exchanging a mentality of lack with a mentality of increase. God has given you the ability to demonstrate great strength in every economic and financial sphere of your life. *Wealth is strength*, and this fact is precisely why Satan despises wealthy children of God.

When God gives you the power to make wealth, He is giving you the ability to be a wealth dynamo. A dynamo is a generator that converts mechanical energy into electrical power. Early generators were known as dynamos, a word derived from the Greek word *dunamis*, which means force or power. A generator converts kinetic motion into electricity as demonstrated in the alternators of automobiles or the massive turbines located within the Hoover Dam. A generator can produce nothing without some form of energy being fed into it. However, a generator will produce exponential power when the proper energy is supplied. The greater the input of energy, the greater the output of power.

The patriarchs of the Bible were wealth generators. They became wealth dynamos – perpetual producers of prosperity — as a result of the massive divine favor that was poured into them. In time, their wealth became a force of power in their lives, their families and their nations. The grace, favor, and blessings of God continually being fed into them served as a catalyst for extraordinary financial increase and abundance.

As wealth and prosperity continue to feed into a Christian dynamo, the result is ever-increasing abundance.

> **Honor the LORD from your wealth**
> **And from the first of all your produce;**
> **So your barns will be filled with plenty**
> **And your vats will overflow with new wine.**
>
> Proverbs 3:9–10

> "Bring the whole tithe into the storehouse, so that there may be food in My house, and test Me now in this," says the LORD of hosts, "if I will not open for you the windows of heaven and pour out for you a blessing until it overflows."
>
> Malachi 3:10

The above scriptures describe a life marked by plenty and overflow. Another word that also has its origins in the Greek word *dunamis* is the English word *dynamic*. The definition of dynamic is, "a force that stimulates change or progress within a system or process. It is something that is highly energetic and active."

When God gave us the power to make wealth — when He made us dynamos — the intention was that we might become financially dynamic. God purposed for His children to be an economic force that stimulates change or progress by tapping into His global wealth system. The natural result is that Christians will become accumulators of abundance, living lives of plenty and overflow.

Abundance Defined

In the same way the sun unleashed the power to create electricity and supercharge the earth's atmosphere, God has unleashed the power for you to create wealth and supercharge your own personal economic atmosphere. Therefore, it is of the utmost importance every child of God understand the divine nature of God's abundance.

Jesus Christ came to seek and save the lost. But He did much more than that:

> **The thief comes only to steal and kill and destroy; I came that they may have life, and have it abundantly. I am the good shepherd; the good shepherd lays down His life for the sheep.**
>
> John 10:10-11

Jesus sacrificed His life so that we might experience abundant life. This is a central tenet of the Lord's gospel and an essential principle of our life of faith.

Perissos is the Greek word for abundance. As an adjective it means greater, excessive, and exceedingly more — beyond anticipation and exceeding expectation. Add to this the definition that abundance is the state of always having a great quantity. Abundance is an extremely plentiful quantity or over-sufficient supply. It is overflowing fullness, affluence, or wealth. To experience abundance is to experience a very great degree of plenteousness, even to a degree that is beyond what is usual.

A life of abundance is a life of unusual plenteousness.

A life of abundance is a life of extraordinary provision.

A life of abundance is a life of remarkable supply.

The abundant life granted to a Christian, bought and paid for with the life of Jesus Christ, is a life that abounds. It is a life that exceeds the ordinary and experiences overflow. It is a life that exudes surplus and goes beyond measure. *Barnes' Notes on the Whole Bible* states, "I am come that they might have life more abundantly — Literally, that they may have abundance, or that which abounds. The word denotes that which is not absolutely essential to life, but which is superadded to make life happy. They shall not merely have life — simple, bare existence — but they shall have all those superadded things which are needful to make that life eminently blessed and happy."

ABUNDANTLY ABOVE

However, it gets even better:

> **Now unto him that is able to do exceeding abundantly above all that we ask or think, according to the power that worketh in us,**
> **Unto him be glory in the church by Christ Jesus throughout all ages, world without end. Amen.**
> **Ephesians 3:20–21 (KJV)**

Huper is the Greek word for "exceeding." It is a preposition that means to go over, beyond, and above. It means to extend benefits that reach beyond the present situation. Exceeding could also be translated as something that works for the advancement of an individual. It is from the Greek word, *huper* that the English word *hyper* is derived. Taken together, *huper perissos*, or hyper abundance, literally means hyper-fullness, hyper-affluence, and hyper-wealth. The intended meaning is that God has enthusiastically, energetically, and excessively deposited abundance into your life!

> **And God is able to bestow every blessing on you in abundance, so that richly enjoying all sufficiency at all times, you may have ample means for all good works.**
> **2 Corinthians 9:8 (WNT)**

Clearly, and unmistakably, the Christian life was designed by God to be a life of advantage!

When a child of God combines the realities of abundance with the character traits of honor, faith, love, humility, worship, wisdom, stewardship, willingness, obedience and generosity, the inevitable result is an advantaged life.

If you are willing and obedient, you will eat the best of the land.

Isaiah 1:19 (BSB)

When all of your bases are covered and all of your needs are supplied, you become positioned in the world to be a force and power for good. It is because you are extraordinarily blessed that you can be an extraordinary blessing.

Paths to Prosperity

Having thoroughly examined the source of our supply and the protection for our provisions, we now turn our attention to the methods of delivery. If you were to ask the average Christian how they believe wealth or increase comes, the majority would respond by saying raises, better jobs, business growth, gifts, or inheritances. Proverbs 14:23 says, "In all labor there is profit," so it should be understood that hard work and persistent effort is essential for increase. While it is true that God frequently uses these more traditional avenues to bless His people, there are other ways that the Lord prospers us as well.

Wealth might come to you through unexpected channels. Wealth might also make its way to you through circumstances or hardships you may not enjoy. For example, there are times where an unexpected job loss leads to a much better paying job. This is what we call a blessing in disguise. In actuality, the Bible shows there are a number of diverse paths to prosperity.

Wealth Is a Crown

We previously examined how Solomon became rich by choosing wisdom over wealth. However, wealth is the result of more than just having right priorities. It is a combination of stewardship, giving, faith, time, patience, ingenuity, and battles. Our spiritual forefathers understood how the prosperity process worked and left for us revelatory examples of what we might expect in our lives.

> **Now these things happened to them as an example, and they were written for our instruction, upon whom the ends of the ages have come.**
>
> **1 Corinthians 10:11**

- Abraham's extraordinary obedience resulted in his extraordinary wealth.

- Jacob's wealth was the result of being cheated by his uncle, Laban.

- The wealth that Joseph eventually enjoyed came as a result of a cruel betrayal.

- David's wealth was amassed as a result of plundering his enemies.

- Solomon inherited massive wealth from his father, David.

- Job's great loss resulted in even greater wealth.

- A king whom God had just judged imparted Daniel's wealth to him.

- The nation of Israel became rich through the process of deliverance.

- Kings gifted wealth to Jesus on the day of His birth.

- Christians receive wealth as their reward for following Jesus

Christ.

Jesus said, "Truly I say to you, there is no one who has left house or brothers or sisters or mother or father or children or farms, for My sake and for the gospel's sake, but that he will receive a hundred times as much now in the present age, houses and brothers and sisters and mothers and children and farms, along with persecutions; and in the age to come, eternal life.

Mark 10:29–30

Remember the Lord Your God

Abundance *from* God should always lead back to generosity *for* God. It is important to note that the house of God, whether it was a tent or a temple, became the focal point of the patriarchs' wealth.

Moreover, because I have set my affection on the house of my God, I have given to the house of my God, over and above all that I have prepared for the holy house, my own special treasure of gold and silver.

1 Chronicles 29:3 (NKJV)

Perhaps the greatest and most well-known example of this found in the Bible was the house that King Solomon built. Detailed and extensive descriptions of the beauty, majesty and wealth of Solomon's Temple have been memorialized in the Old Testament books of 1 Kings and 2 Chronicles. Wealth has always been associated with and closely connected to God's temples and was prominent in both its furnishings and construction. Even when God's houses were completed, wealth continued to pour in through the offerings of His people.

The Treasure House

> **"Bring the whole tithe into the storehouse, so that there may be food in My house, and test Me now in this," says the LORD of hosts, "if I will not open for you the windows of heaven and pour out for you a blessing until it overflows."**
>
> **Malachi 3:10**

Ostar, the Hebrew word referring to God's "storehouse," literally means *treasury-house*. Taking this into consideration, the first line of this verse could read, "Bring the whole tithe into the treasury-house." The Hebrew word for "tithes" means a tenth, and the Hebrew word for offering means, "a spontaneous gift, present, or sacrifice."

Additionally, Jesus taught that the house of God is where our tithes and offerings are sanctified:

> **"You fools and blind men! Which is more important, the gold or the temple that sanctified the gold?"**
>
> **Matthew 23:17**

Barnes' Notes on the Whole Bible states, "To sanctify is to make holy. The gold had no holiness but what it derived from the temple. If in any other place, it would be no more holy than any other gold." The *Geneva Bible* says, "The temple causes the gold which is dedicated to a holy use to be considered holy." Giving to God's house supercharges your gifts!

The Apostle Paul taught that mortal men on the earth receive tithes, but Jesus Christ, Who is our High Priest, also receives tithes in heaven. The church exists in both heaven and on the earth. It is a supernatural house that encapsulates heaven (where gold originated) to the earth (where gold is deposited). Because God's economic system is universal, what is released in heaven is also released on the earth.

I will give you the keys of the kingdom of heaven; and whatever you bind on earth shall have been bound in heaven, and whatever you loose on earth shall have been loosed in heaven.

Matthew 16:19

Tithes and offerings are, in part, a deposit on the earth and, in part, a transfer to heaven. Our gifts are a transfer of value back to God made as an act of our love and appreciation for His goodness. Giving and receiving works much like the concept of supply and demand. God's supply, or His blessings, puts a demand on the giver while the giver's offering puts a demand on the supply. The church (storehouse or treasury-house) is a miraculous facility because it both receives supply and meets demand.

Giving is what triggers the opening of windows in heaven. The word "window" can be somewhat misleading to the average person because it paints the picture of a simple or common opening in the side of a building. But the Hebrew word for "windows" in Malachi 3:10 is *arubbah*. The word describes a sluice and is also correctly translated as *floodgate*. A sluice is a sliding gate or other such device for controlling the flow of water. A floodgate is a restraint system designed to hold back an outpouring of something powerful or substantial. It is the same word used in Genesis 7:11 to describe the "floodgates of the sky" being opened at the time of the great flood in the life of Noah. Together, these terms describe a directional channel that regulates the release and flow of something powerful.

Tithes and offerings will always open a floodgate of blessings. The pouring out of these various blessings come with great force and in such quantity, they are difficult to measure and contain. The blessing of God brings protection, preservation, and exponential increase into our lives. And since God has designed our giving to affect the future as well, it allows us the opportunity to address financial problems that have not yet arisen.

> **Give, and it shall be given unto you; good measure, pressed down, and shaken together, and running over, shall men give into your bosom. For with the same measure that ye mete withal it shall be measured to you again.**
>
> **Luke 6:38 (KJV)**

Giving connects heaven's abundance with earth's needs.

Giving paves the runway for increase.

Giving carves out new avenues of continuing increase.

Tithing opens the gate of heaven.

> **Then Jacob awoke from his sleep and said, "Surely the LORD is in this place, and I did not know it." He was afraid and said, "How awesome is this place! This is none other than the house of God, and this is the gate of heaven.**
>
> **This stone, which I have set up as a pillar, will be God's house, and of all that You give me I will surely give a tenth to You."**
>
> **Genesis 28:16–17, 22**

There is no offering so supernaturally blessed as the one that comes into the house of God!

THE AUTHORITY TO PROSPER

The Crown of Wealth carries with it the rights to prosper. Prospering literally means continual growth in success, and it is continual prosperity that creates permanent wealth.

You are the reason God put gold in the earth.

You are the reason God put wealth in the world.

You are the reason God created a global wealth system.

You are the reason God created a crown of wealth.

The divine laws that govern biblical wealth, prosperity, and increase will radically transform you, because, as a child of God, you have been empowered to experience a life of abundance, financial freedom, and economic advantage.

It is time to take action.

Wealth is your crown!

Conclusion

When it comes to the supremely important topic of divine wealth, the words of God are the only words that should matter. And "Good measure, pressed down, shaken together, and running over" is the exact phrase Jesus Christ used to illustrate the lives of those who understand and activate the laws of wealth, prosperity, abundance, and increase. His words describe the financial reward system each and every Christian has been invited to experience and enjoy. Financial blessing is always the natural result of understanding how and why biblical wealth works.

The power and providence of wealth is demonstrably woven throughout Scripture. Consequently, the inescapable conclusion is that wealth — along with all its wonderful derivatives — are intended to be a part of the Christian's life while upon the earth. The totality of scriptures, from Genesis to Revelation, paints a very different picture of wealth than most hold today. In truth, there has never been such a thing as a "prosperity movement." There has only ever been, and will only ever be, a *prosperity reality*.

In the book of Genesis, over the course of six majestic days, God spoke into existence light, the sky, land, thriving vegetation, and all living creatures. On the sixth day He fashioned Adam from the dust of the ground, formed Eve out of Adam's rib, and placed the two of them in the garden of Eden. God blessed them, surrounding them with good and pleasant things, and welcomed them to enjoy dominion over all the earth. God concluded each day by pronouncing His efforts as "good." Finally, on the seventh day, God rested from all His work.

It was not by coincidence that God placed gold in Eden and then placed man next to that very gold. In fact, gold was the very first thing God pronounced as good following the account of creation. God gave humanity a home, companionship, generous provisions, and great wealth. What was true then and there still holds true here and now.

God's design for the garden of Eden was that it would be a place of peace, presence, power, and prosperity. From that place, Adam and Eve were charged to subdue the earth, which included gold — or wealth — and exercise dominion over it. Not only does the story of mankind's divine provision begin with the gold of Eden, it continues and is expanded upon with vast quantities of gold in heaven. According to Revelation 21:15-21, the New Jerusalem, along with the streets of the holy city, consist of pure gold. These are vivid reminders for us that God is not only the King of saints, but also the King of wealth. Just as mankind's birth on the earth began with wealth, his or her future in eternity will continue alongside wealth as well, their habitation being a city literally made of solid gold.

Why would the Lord entwine His people's past and future with wealth, yet not their present-day lives? The here and now is when we need it. *The here and now is when we can utilize it and make the most difference.* The reality is that wealth has always been both divinely and providentially connected to God's people. There is no reason that, in modern times, it shouldn't be received and enjoyed as the same. When a person considers the divine origins of wealth, taken together with the prominent role it plays in eternity, the inevitable conclusion must be that wealth is a biblical sign of God's blessing and endorsement.

Conclusion

Every Christian has been endowed with royal rights to experience a life of prosperity, abundance, and increase. This is why Proverbs 14:24 states, "Wealth is a crown." The wisdom for biblical wealth will work throughout the world, no matter where it is heard or when it is put into practice. For thousands of years, no matter where God's people have journeyed throughout the earth, they have discovered wealth waiting there for them.

You have been empowered to enjoy a life of abundance, financial freedom, and economic superiority. God does not show favoritism or partiality, and He makes no distinction between one person and another.

What the Lord did for others, He will also do for you.

www.ingramcontent.com/pod-product-compliance
Lightning Source LLC
LaVergne TN
LVHW051836080426
835512LV00018B/2914